INFLUENCING AND COLLABORATING FOR RESULTS

DUKE CORPORATE EDUCATION

LEADING
FROM THE
CENTER

INFLUENCING AND COLLABORATING FOR RESULTS

Dearborn™
Trade Publishing
A **Kaplan Professional** Company

President, Dearborn Publishing: Roy Lipner
Vice President and Publisher: Cynthia A. Zigmund
Acquisitions Editor: Jonathan Malysiak
Senior Project Editor: Trey Thoelcke
Interior Design: Lucy Jenkins
Cover Design: Design Solutions
Typesetting: Elizabeth Pitts

Published by Dearborn Trade Publishing
A Kaplan Professional Company

Printed in the United States of America

05 06 07 10 9 8 7 6 5 4 3 2 1

Library of Congress Cataloging-in-Publication Data

Duke Corporate Education.
    Influencing and collaborating for results / Duke Corporate Education.
        p.   cm. — (Leading from the center)
    Includes bibliographical references and index.
    ISBN 0-7931-9521-7
    1. Strategic alliances (Business) 2. Business networks. I. Title. II. Series.
    HD69.S8D85 2005
    658'.044—dc22

                                                                2005002824

CONTENTS

ACKNOWLEDGMENTS

First and foremost, we want to thank our clients and the many program participants around the globe. We begin our work by listening to our clients and gaining an understanding of their business challenges. Working with talented clients and actively engaging in their challenges across a range of industries and geographies has afforded us the opportunity to learn and develop an informed point of view on these topics. We thank our clients for trusting in our approach and making us part of their team.

We are also fortunate to have an extensive network of faculty, coaches, facilitators, and partners who believe in our mission and have opted to join in our adventure. Together, we have delivered programs in 37 different countries since we formed in July 2000. We absolutely could not have accomplished what we have and learned what we know without them.

John Tolsma and his colleagues at erroyo have been close partners for several years. As John worked with us, he came to believe that we have something unique to say and urged us to capture our ideas in these books. He introduced us to our editors at Dearborn Trade and the rest, as they say, is history. Jon Malysiak became our first publishing contact. He and the rest of the Dearborn team have patiently guided us through this process. We can't thank them enough.

As with any organization, we too have created a shorthand that accelerates our own conversation, but doesn't translate well outside Duke CE. We were lucky to have the writing and editing assistance of a local writer, Elizabeth Brack. Betsy worked with us over the many versions and edits of these chapters to make the words flow more smoothly.

Many members of the Duke CE family were willing to share their experiences, their personal stories and their (scarce) time in helping us through this process. We especially thank Gil McWilliam and Deb

Stout for their invaluable input. In spite of hectic travel and long days, they managed to find time in the margins to help by reading, editing and sometimes rewriting our thoughts.

Throughout the book you will see several graphical images reinforcing the surrounding ideas. Ryan Stevens worked with us patiently to capture our thoughts and ideas into the graphical images included within the book; often working with vague instructions such as—it should feel like 'this.' He did a wonderful job.

Without a doubt the busiest person at Duke CE, our CEO Blair Sheppard, was instrumental to this effort. He supported the initiative from the outset and more importantly always made time to review our output and guide our thinking. His assistance is without measure. We could not have done it without him.

During the many weeks we've spent working on this book—engaging clients, researching, talking, writing, editing, and then cycling back to the beginning—we came across a statement one day that essentially said no great works (musical compositions, novels, and the like) can be created by a team—the thought being that they require the guiding vision and creativity of a single, uniquely talented individual. Although our book certainly isn't in the category of "great literary works," we take immense pride that this, like our client work, has been indeed very much a team effort.

We've drawn upon the insight, experience, and expertise from numerous colleagues here at Duke CE. We hope that the content of this book stimulates your thinking and improves your ability to act and solve the challenges confronting you.

The *Influencing and Collaborating for Results* book team: Michael Canning, Marla Tuchinsky, Cindy Campbell, and Kati Clement-Frazier.

INTRODUCTION

In the past 30 years, they have been repeatedly laid off, outsourced, replaced by information technology applications, and insulted with such derogatory names as "the cement layer." Their bosses accused them of distorting and disrupting communication in their organizations, and their subordinates accused them of thwarting the subordinates' autonomy and empowerment. Who are "they"? Middle managers, those managing in the middle of the organization.

With such treatment, you might think that middle managers are villainous evildoers who sabotage companies, or obstructionist bureaucrats who stand in the way of real work getting done. However, the reality is just the opposite. When performed well, the middle manager role is critical in organizations.

Although over the past several decades the value and stature of middle managers has seen both high and low points, we at Duke Corporate Education believe that managing in the center of the organization has always been both critically important and personally demanding. As one would expect, the essence of the role—the required mind-set and skill set—has continued to change over time. The need to update each of these dimensions is driven by periodic shifts in such underlying forces as marketplace dynamics, technology, organizational structure, and employee expectations. Now and then, these forces converge to create a point of inflection that calls for a "step change" in how organizations are governed, with particular implications for those managing in the center.

In the *Leading from the Center* series, we examine some of these primary causes that are shaping what it means to successfully lead from the center in the modern organization. We outline the emerging imperative for middle management in an organization as well as the mind-set, knowledge, and skills required to successfully navigate through the most prevalent challenges that lie ahead.

THE NEW CENTER

There are four powerful and pervasive trends affecting the role that managers in the center of an organization are being asked to assume. These trends—information technology, industry convergence, globalization, and regulations—connect directly to the challenges these managers are facing.

Compared to twenty or thirty years ago, *information technology* has escalated the amount, speed, and availability of data, to the point that it has changed the way we work and live. Access to information has shifted more power to our customers and suppliers. They not only have more information, but are directly involved in and interacting with the various processes along the value chain. On a personal level, we now find ourselves connected to other people all the time; cell phones, pagers, BlackBerrys, and PDAs all reinforce the 24/7 culture. The transition from work week to weekend and back is less distinct. These micro-transitions happen all day, every day because many of us remain connected all the time.

Industries previously seen as separate are now seeing multiple points of *convergence*. Think about how digital technology has led to a convergence of sound, image, text, computing, and communications. Longstanding industry boundaries and parameters are gone (e.g., cable television companies are in the phone business, electronics companies sell music), and along with them, the basis and nature of competition. The boundaries are blurred. It's clear that new possibilities, opportunities, and directions exist, but it isn't always clear what managers should do. Managers will have to be prepared to adapt; their role is to observe, learn from experience, and set direction dynamically. Layered on top of this is the need to manage a more complex set of relationships—cooperating on Monday, competing on Tuesday, and partnering on Wednesday.

Globalization means that assets are now distributed and configured around the world to serve customers and gain competitive advantage. Even companies that consider themselves local interact with global organizations. There is more reliance on fast-developing regional centers of expertise. For example, computer programming in India and manufacturing in China. This means that middle managers are interacting with and coordinating the efforts of people who live in different cultures, and may be awake while the managers are asleep. The notion of a workday has changed as the work straddles time zones. The nature of leading has changed as it becomes more common to partner with vendors and work in virtual teams across regions.

The first three forces are causing shifts in the fourth—the *regulatory environment*. Many industries are experiencing more regulation, while a few others are experiencing less. In some arenas now experiencing more regulation, there is also a drive for more accountability. Demand for more accountability leads to a greater desire to clarify boundaries and roles. Yet there is more ambiguity as to what the rules are and how best to operationalize them. Consider how, in the wake of Sarbanes-Oxley legislation, U.S. companies and their accountants continue to sort through the new requirements, while rail companies in Britain are negotiating which company is responsible for maintaining what stretch of tracks. Middle managers sit where regulations get implemented, and are a critical force in shaping how companies respond to the shifts in the environment.

All of these changes have implications for those managing at the center of organizations. No small group at the top can have the entire picture because the environment has more of everything: more information and connectivity, a faster pace, a dynamic competitive space, greater geographic reach, better informed and connected customers and suppliers, and shifting legal rules of the game. No small group can process the implications, make thoughtful decisions and disseminate clear action steps. The top of the organization needs those in the center to help make sense of the dynamic environment. The connection between strategy development and strategy execution becomes less linear and more interdependent and, therefore, managers in the center become pivotal actors.

As we said earlier, the notion of the middle of an organization typically conjures up a vertical image depicting managers in the center of a hierarchy. This mental image carries with it a perception of those managers as gatekeepers—controlling the pace at which information or resources flow down or up. It appears to be simple and linear.

However, as many of you are no doubt experiencing, you now find yourselves navigating in a matrix, and as a node in a network or

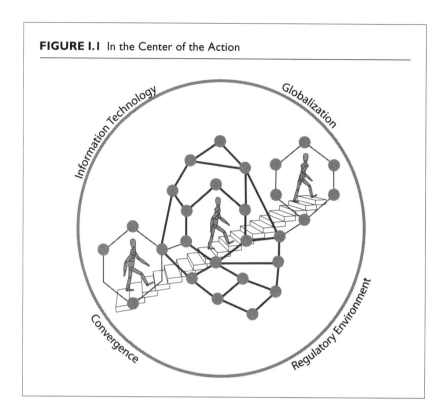

FIGURE I.1 In the Center of the Action

multiple networks. As depicted in Figure I.1, this new view of the
center conjures up images of centrality, integration, connection, and
catalyst. *You are in the center of the action, not the middle of a hierarchy.*
When you overlay this connected view on the traditional vertical notion, it produces some interesting tensions, trade offs, and opportunities. Your formal authority runs vertically, but your real power to
achieve results stems from your ability to work across all levels and
boundaries.

IF YOU ARE LEADING FROM THE CENTER

If you are a manager in the center today, you have many hats to
wear, more balls to juggle and fewer certainties in your work environment. You have to be adaptive yet provide continuity in your leadership. You need to simultaneously translate strategy, influence and
collaborate, lead teams, coach and motivate, support innovation and

own the systems and processes—all in the service of getting results. Those in the center need more courage than ever. You are the conscience of your organizations, carrying forth the values, and at the same time you build today and tomorrow's business success.

Strategy Translator

As a strategy translator, you must first understand the corporate strategy and determine what parts of it your group can best support. Next, you must translate it into an action plan for your group, making sure it aligns well to the overall strategy. You'll need to consider which projects are essential stepping stones and which are needed in their own right, and establish some priorities or guiding goals. You must then communicate the details of the plan and priorities, and create momentum around them. As your team implements, you'll need to involve not only your people but to also collaborate and coordinate with others, including peers, customers, and other units. Instead of directing a one way downward flow of information, you must translate upward as well and act as a conduit for strategic feedback to the executives above.

Influencer and Collaborator for Results

Middle managers must learn how to make things happen by influencing, integrating, and collaborating across the boundaries of the organization. As a manager, instead of focusing exclusively on your piece, you have to look outside of your own group to develop a network of supporting relationships. Rather than issuing commands and asserting power based on your position, you have to use other tactics to gain agreement and make things happen.

Leader of Teams

Teams have become a one-size-fits-all solution for organizing work in today's economy—virtual teams, project teams, product teams, and function-specific teams—and can be either the blessing or the bane of many companies. Your role as a manager includes understanding the challenges of teams and facilitating their development so that they can be effective more quickly. You have to align the team's energy and talents in a way that will deliver the desired results. You are responsible for creating an environment that will help this group of people work well together to achieve today's objectives and to develop the skills needed to take on future goals.

Coach and Motivator

Many organizations are well positioned to execute their strategies in yesterday's environment, they are moderately able to meet their current needs, and often they are not thinking about how to position themselves for the future. From the center of the organization, middle managers assume much of the responsibility for their people. They create an environment to attract and retain good employees, coach them to do their current jobs better, and bear primary responsibility for developing others. As a manager, you must figure out how to build the next level of capability, protect existing people, connect their aspirations to opportunities for development, and make work more enjoyable. You need to provide regular feedback—both positive and redirecting—and build strong relationships with those who surround you. If done well, your departments will be more efficient and your employees will be better equipped to become leaders in their own right.

Intrapreneur/Innovator

Enabling and supporting an innovative approach within your company will foster the strategic direction of the future. To effectively sponsor innovation, you need to create the context for your people, foster a climate that supports innovative efforts, and actively sponsor the ideas of the future. You have to *be* innovative and *lead* the innovative efforts of others. Innovation is most often associated with new-product development, but innovative approaches also are needed in developing new services or solving internal system and process problems. As a manager, you use their influence and relationships to find the root cause of problems, and the resources to make change happen.

Owner of Systems and Processes

You need to understand that part of your role is to take ownership for architecting new systems and processes. You will have to shift your thinking from living within existing systems and processes to making sure that those systems and processes work well: Do the systems and processes support or get in the way of progress? One of the mistakes we have made in the past is to not hold managers accountable for their role in architecting the next generation of systems and processes. As a manager, you must perform harsh audits of existing systems, and understand when to tear down what may have been left in place from a past strategy. You need to assess what is no longer relevant and/or is no longer working. Part of your responsibility is to think about and decide whether to reengineer or remove existing systems.

SHIFT IN MIND-SET NEEDED FOR THE FUTURE

As you approach each of the challenges of leading from the center of your organization, you may need to shift your mind-set. As we've noted, the world is more complex and interconnected than before, and you and other middle managers can't be successful without support and resources throughout the organization. The highest value solutions will depend on their ability to interact across boundaries and understand the interdependencies of projects and initiatives. This includes not just the connectedness of such things as systems and processes, but also the people associated with the project and their interests.

Initiating compelling communications will be a core shift as you interact with others, including bosses, teams, peers, and clients. The shift is toward a more interactive communication that includes inquiring about what others see as important, what problems they face, and what mental models they are working from. As you interact across boundaries and generate good conversations, the focus will not be on "winning" the single negotiation or completing the single project, but on building sustainable relationships and solutions for the future.

Over the next eight chapters, we'll walk you through a planning process that takes you from identifying your stakeholders to building a sustained network of relationships and solutions for your organization.

CHAPTER ONE

UNDERSTANDING INFLUENCE AND COLLABORATION

IN THIS CHAPTER

Understanding Influence and Collaboration ■ Strong Networks Make Strong Managers ■ Influence and Collaboration in Today's Workplace ■ Making Things Happen: A New Mind-Set for Managers

What does effective influence look like in today's business world? Why is it imperative to getting results? How can collaboration be used to maximize your impact?

How many times have you heard that solutions need to be both fast "and" systemic, high quality "and" cost effective? Managing in the age of "and" demands that managers think, act, and interact differently to get things done and create value. It quickly becomes apparent that yesterday's perspective, skills, and approaches are no longer adequate. A fresh approach is called for, one that enables you as a manager to effectively navigate through this dynamic territory and create compelling reasons for others to join you in developing and implementing powerful solutions for your company and your customers.

In today's fast-paced, complex business environment, managers are simultaneously facing elaborate challenges and greater pressure to make the right things happen and achieve the desired business results. Shaping and executing sustainable solutions in a dynamic en-

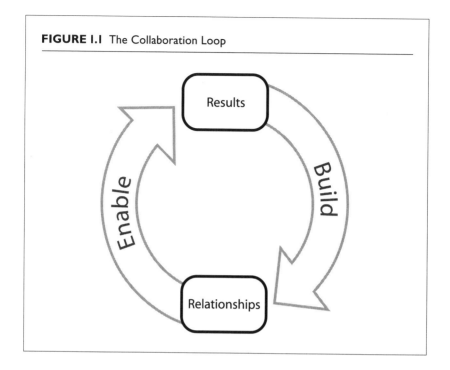

FIGURE 1.1 The Collaboration Loop

vironment laden with uncertainty and paradoxes isn't easy. Leading from the center of an organization today, regardless of the size, is more challenging than ever.

To get those results, managers need to collaborate with others. It can become a virtuous cycle: producing results leads to credibility, confidence, and trust in relationship partners. Increased trust and respect lead to the partner being more willing and open to collaborating again and achieving results. Over time, it becomes easier to work together and more efficiently get the outcomes you want.

UNDERSTANDING INFLUENCE AND COLLABORATION

influence (noun): *the act or power of producing an effect without apparent exertion of force or direct exercise of command;* (transitive verb): *to affect or alter by indirect or intangible means*

While Webster's definition of influence hasn't changed, the dominant interpretation and associated management practices in the business world have evolved. By way of example, let's compare three time periods and the dominant interpretation and practice of influence in the corporate setting:

1. During the first half of the 20th century, at the height of the Industrial Revolution, businesses tended to be managed through downward communication and control. Managers in this period exerted influence through the use of power, primarily positional power. The result: The emergence of unions and the trend toward vertical integration.

2. In the last quarter of the 20th century, expectations of the workforce were elevated. People developed organizations, and implemented processes and practices to facilitate change. Managers in the middle were schooled that influence meant involving and engaging people to reduce the resistance to the desired change. Although this was certainly a step forward, the dominant lesson was that you can't simply tell people what to do—they need to feel included.

3. Today, in a world where no one holds the complete picture and there is no single right answer, actively engaging people is not a social nicety, but rather it is an imperative to understanding the current situation or opportunity and enriching the quality of the solution. We've learned that effective management is enhanced by understanding and using influence and collaboration to achieve work solutions.

collaboration (noun): *the act of working together; united labor;* (intransitive verb): *to work jointly with others or together especially in an intellectual endeavor*

STRONG NETWORKS MAKE STRONG MANAGERS

Why are influence and collaboration an imperative for middle managers in today's business world? Simply put, you can't do it alone. To be effective today, managers must collaborate across and beyond the borders of the organization, building the connections and relationships that will be the pathways to achieving their goals. Without a strong network of relationships and the ability to collaborate with others, producing successful results is nearly impossible. A strong network makes a strong manager.

For example, a large IT and communications solutions organization has now become a fiercely effective competitor in the outsourcing business in the United Kingdom. Two years ago, they were on the brink of foreclosure. Their approach to IT management had become stale and they were losing market share at an alarming rate. But, like many great companies before them, instead of leaving the business and refocusing efforts in other parts of the world, they decided to completely reshape their business model. At the heart of this effort was a decision to focus on continuously realigning their approach to a client: to not be just a mechanism for outsourcing non-core activities within the IT world, but to be a source of competitive advantage for their customers.

Their approach went so far as radically altering their approach to a client's business in the middle of a contract, when the client's environment and strategic needs shifted. Better to put yourself out of business than have someone else do it. This shift in approach to the business has been remarkably successful. The company has been the fastest growing player in the outsourcing business two years in a row. At the heart of this strategy is the account team manager. For the model to work, an account manager needs to be able to:

- Get access to senior people at the client firm in order to truly understand their business needs, rather than continue to interact solely with the technology partner with whom they are comfortable.
- Build a set of relationships with others in the client's industry to understand where the challenges for the client are truly evolving.
- Bring a team of actors together within the company to create a truly novel and value enhancing approach to the client's emerging needs.
- Bring the full resources of the company to bear in building a sustainable answer.

Unfortunately, very few of these actors live within the account manager's chain of command. The account manager is instead a catalyst or orchestrator of a set of resources that have many other opportunities available to them for how to spend their time and effort.

Let's look at a large nongovernmental organization with a storied history of having dropped food packages to people in need in times of war, civil uprising, and famine. Their organization is now synonymous with all sorts of survival packages, including what parents send children at camp or college to convey love and concern. But, the NGO's world too has changed. At the heart of the shift has been what they consider a best solution for people in times of need.

Except in the most episodic and extreme disasters, such as the 2004 Indian Ocean tsunami, the largest need is not for temporary food provisions, but assistance moving to self-sufficiency. To coin an old phrase, their most value-enhancing role is not to provide fish to the hungry, but instead to teach them how to fish. This requires a dramatic shift in the role of the country managers within their organization. Their task is to identify projects with the greatest likelihood of enhancing the welfare of a community, region, or country, and convene the resources necessary to get the project started and sustained. In a sense, the country managers have shifted from leading a large scale, self-contained logistics operation to heading a set of people who insinuate themselves into a community to facilitate, convene, and support long-term self-guided initiatives. The goal of most projects is to transfer control of the work to the indigenous population as quickly as possible. This shift in focus has required a huge shift in the orientation of the country manager and all of the staff within the NGO.

Other examples abound.

- A VP at a major pharmaceutical firm has been asked to begin looking at how the clinical trial process could be made more efficient and has been given six months to come up with a solution that can be implemented. The company simply can't afford the present process. However, beyond those rather nebulous instructions, she heard no specific mandates outlined, nor did she gain additional resources. She was simply told to go use her great talents to work it out.

- A controller within an organization is finalizing the implementation of a major IT installation within his company and a large portion of his team has just taken seriously ill.
- The CFO of a midsize company needs to raise capital from a new set of resources for a key initiative and the terms of the deal matter a great deal.

Classically, the protagonists in each of these examples would have resolved their problems by working up a chain of command to argue for money, personnel, resources, and a mandate, or down a chain of command to get those working for them to perform the necessary tasks. In each case, to take this approach would fail them. The account manager in the information technology organization needs resources that only meet at the level of the CEO (who just does not have the time or inclination to make such a decision) or they exist entirely outside of the company's walls. The country managers at the NGO need to become a part of the fabric of their country, able to efficiently convene and facilitate large clusters of often hostile players. The pharmaceutical VP is expected by her employer to come up with the approach, resources, and mandate through her own talents. The controller does not have the time to work the system for resources; he has a crisis now. The CFO's firm needs a new set of relationships; she cannot depend on those her boss or employees already have.

Interestingly, in life more broadly we do not need to go to a chain of command to get such problems resolved. The answer lies in the network of relations we draw on for information, social support, or other resources: dealing with significant loss such as the death of a loved one, job loss, or divorce; finding much-needed information; gaining access to resources; raising money. We all have learned to depend on networks of relationships in times of need. Research has generally shown that those who have strong networks of support respond to life's challenges more effectively, live longer and happier lives, and are generally more successful and healthy (Cohen, 2004).

The same is true in organizations. (Cross, 2004) Network resources are critical for dealing with a range of problems, including those of the managers we've seen in the previous examples. This book is focused on how those in the middle can play within this web of mutually adaptive network actors to effectively perform their role.

The term *mutual* is the key to success in a networked world. Much of the advice on getting things done in organizations is built on a unilateral view of influence. Your job as a middle manager is to use all the influence resources at your command—from authority, to persuasion, to money, to expertise, to attraction—to get your task done.

In the view adopted in this book, however, engagement is much more mutual. While drawing on others to work on tasks or projects that are important to you, it is essential to recognize that you are creating an obligation to be available to them. You are required to create an offer that meets their needs as well as your own. Each actor in a network assists the others, blurring the lines of supplier and customer, boss and employee, and asker and answerer. Managers are not just *in* the middle, they are *of* the middle, involved in a network of continuously adapting peers.

Like the companies in which we are employed, our relationships are more complex and more dynamic than they used to be. We need to learn how to work within those relationships, because it is through projects or tasks that we build and apply networks. Each allows the other to happen.

First let's consider how to make projects work, and then consider how to use the relationships we developed—one task or project at a time—in a broader sense. We start with the principles that will serve as the basis for all that will follow, so let's introduce them here and return to them at the end of this book.

1. *Keep good company.* Each of us can remember hearing from our parents, or saying as parents, that the company you keep matters. This phrase refers to the influence that peers have on us as we develop our view of the world and of us within that world. Our network is a source of information, reference, and identity. However, in today's business world, the company you keep is important for several other reasons. Your ability to perform difficult tasks is limited by the range of resources you can draw on when needed. The CFO needs to know a set of bankers who will take the time to help her with a challenging financing issue. The controller needs friends with technical and managerial skill who owe him a favor and are willing to work long hours to help him meet his deadline.

The pharmaceutical VP needs people who can help her discern where to begin and how to think about the challenge she's been handed. The company you keep holds relationships, knowledge, and counsel.

2. *Build goodwill.* Knowing people is not sufficient. It is also necessary to have a reservoir of goodwill to draw on when you need their help. Goodwill helps another to want to listen to your offer, request, or suggestion. It makes it more likely the other will return your call instead of a dozen others. It helps smooth rough patches as you work through getting a project started, and tackle tough conversations that are inevitable in fast-paced, interdependent work. Goodwill comes through the creation of a shared sense of the future, a shared identity, and investment in the other, but goodwill is built over time. What happens if the IT account manager visits those in other divisions for the first time when he needs a new approach to *his* client? They are unlikely to pay much attention to his request, consider his need for a new approach sensible, or trust him to deliver on his end of any understanding. Building goodwill is tricky: You do not know who you may need to depend on for any given task or project until the project is understood, yet you have to build goodwill in advance. Thus, being conscious of the company you keep is essential for developing goodwill and truly generating long-term value for both of you.

3. *Engage.* Relationships are built through joint activity. Joint activity increases our understanding of one another; builds a common identity through shared experiences, shared hardship, and ongoing interaction; and creates a sense of mutual obligation for future interaction. It also establishes patterns of interaction that make future engagements easier and allows each party to learn to depend on the other to get important work done. If goodwill is the heart of a relationship, engagement is the muscle fiber. Moreover, engagement is what makes relationships valuable and fun. Through work, projects, advice, information sharing, and informal activity, relationships develop depth and texture. Through engagement we come to know more about ourselves and our net-

work of relations. Finally, engagement is to extend our set of relationships and deepen and strengthen our network.

4. *Invest in and sustain trust.* In network transactions, typical forms of managerial control to ensure that others do as needed do not exist. Sometimes there is a contract with sanctions implied in the agreement; sometimes people share a boss in common. In either instance, invoking the penalty clause or the boss is the last step you should take. Instead, it is essential to create trustworthiness within the parties in a network. This requires significant investment from all involved. Without trustworthiness, exchanges don't occur reliably or effectively. In networks, business is literally done on a handshake.

5. *Make the connections.* Operating from the center implies a certain duty to make connections and act as an integrator. In terms of the work, it's important to identify and understand the upstream, downstream, and lateral interdependencies associated with the initiatives or projects you are leading. With respect to the people, it's imperative that you connect and engage the right set of people, and manage in a way that simultaneously advances the desired results and relationships. This requires you as a manager to think and act more systemically.

We will come back to these principles later. For now, consider that whatever you do as a manager in the center of an organization, managing relationships will be critical to getting results.

INFLUENCE AND COLLABORATION IN TODAY'S WORKPLACE

Given the interdependencies and complexities in today's workplace, the topic of influence requires a new lens. Let's revisit Webster's definition and consider how it applies to today's workplace. Today, influencing in this interconnected business world is less about command and control and more about bringing the right elements together to get results. It's definition might be rephrased as the following:

influence (noun): *the art or skill of getting work done indirectly*

Prior notions around the topic of influence should be expanded to incorporate the need for collaboration. Approaching influence through a collaborative frame will enable you to build the relationships necessary to sustain an effective network of people. Collaboration might be redefined as the following:

collaboration (noun): *working cooperatively, sharing knowledge and experience, in order to achieve a collective goal*

Consider the definition of influence and stretch your memory back to Chemistry 101 to recall the role of the catalyst. A catalyst is an element that induces or accelerates a reaction without being consumed by the reaction itself. This is your role as a middle manager—the role of a catalyst. As a manager, it is your responsibility to create the compelling context and guide the experiment—to bring the elements together, elicit an intended reaction, measure that reaction, and manage the upstream and downstream effects.

MAKING THINGS HAPPEN
A New Mind-Set for Managers

Today's manager must be focused on creating viable solutions and value for the company. You need to incorporate a new way of thinking in the development of solutions and processes. The best result isn't one that considers only the implications and benefits for your group. To achieve the best, sustainable results, you have to consider the interdependencies, connections, and long-term implications across the entire organization. Consider the following:

- How will a certain initiative affect other parts of the organization—from the top, from the bottom?
- What are the intended consequences?
- What unintended consequences could result?
- Who in particular will be affected—employees, customers, vendors, partners?
- How will the initiative be supported and executed?
- How will the right environment be created to foster the desired result?

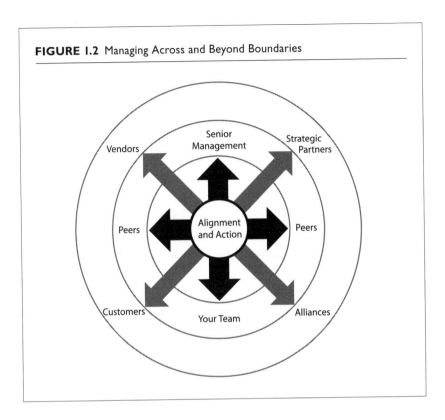

FIGURE 1.2 Managing Across and Beyond Boundaries

Before you can answer these and similar questions, you have to understand what it means to "lead from the center." As shown in Figure 1.2, this concept integrates what it means to be a manager—you reach out above, below, across, and beyond boundaries to develop solutions to challenges. These are the people who make up your stakeholders—the people with whom you will create solutions to problems and advance the company's mission.

Managers have to consider the consequences of the solutions they are building: How will a new product impact the current work structure? What impact will a change in process have on subsequent processes and products? The "A plus B leads to C" approach no longer applies. By taking an approach that considers how a solution will impact the system as a whole, you will be able to increase your effectiveness and value to the company.

Managers need the support and interaction of colleagues, employees, and upper management to get projects accomplished. By *exerting influence and collaborating,* you can increase alignment and action to achieve goals across all levels—from senior management, through your team and direct reports, and laterally with peers and other divisions within the company. It's not about promoting your own agenda—influence is about connecting with people, building a common understanding, and working together to generate a desired outcome for the organization and your stakeholders.

Shifting the way you think about achieving short-term results to a new emphasis on building relationships is also necessary. Building long-term relationships with coworkers, management, customers, vendors, and others is more important than ever. To achieve your goals and produce results, you have to build and nurture relationships, which will increase your understanding of more complex issues as well as your ability to influence others.

But how do you get there? By building relationships—beginning with effective communication, which leads to understanding, commitment, and trust—ultimately leading to alignment and results.

Influencing involves collaboration. By collaborating with your stakeholders, you can create a high-value solution that incorporates not just your ideas, but their ideas, experiences, and expertise. Think of the give-and-take aspect of a friendship or other nonwork relationship—it involves a high degree of back-and-forth, learning how to work together, and learning about past experiences that can impact your current challenge. By developing your connections with stakeholders, you gain insights that will increase the likelihood of developing a high-value solution.

Influencing results is a cyclical, iterative process—a process you can use throughout anything you do. It involves:

- Understanding your network
- Connecting with colleagues
- Creating the invitation
- Developing a story
- Tailoring the message
- Creating a shared story
- Building credibility

We'll explore each of these in the following chapters.

CHAPTER TWO

MAPPING YOUR NETWORK

IN THIS CHAPTER

Who Are Stakeholders? ■ Using the Stakeholder
Map ■ How the Stakeholder Map Works ■ The Manager's
Challenge ■ Building Your Stakeholder Map

In addition to the daily tasks of just doing business, as a manager you likely have responsibility for larger objectives and "special projects" that are critical to the company's strategic direction. You and your team are expected to deliver results. One CEO often compares the manager's task of influencing and collaborating for results to that of party host. One of the first tasks is to think about the guest list and then create a compelling invitation that will make people want to be a part of the event. Think about the largest party that you organized and hosted, then add 100 to the guest list. Now add 1,000. It becomes obvious pretty quickly that you can't do it alone.

In today's workplace, you also can't produce results alone. Most likely, you have some idea about how to proceed with some of the challenges that you've been given. In the old days of "command and control" management, you might have presented a solution and expected it to be implemented. Only later would you find out what that solution's impact had on the company, its employees, its customers, and beyond—or whether it actually was the best solution, and one that would be sustainable for some time to come. This try-and-see approach might deliver successful results for the company, but it might also implement solutions with unintended negative effects, solutions that are at odds with the work of other projects, or solutions that are not sustainable given the company's strategic direction.

Now, with the emphasis shifting to a more indirect and collaborative management style, managers no longer have to find the solution to the problem themselves; however, they do have to identify and cultivate an extensive network of stakeholders who will facilitate collaboration and craft the best solutions for the company.

WHO ARE STAKEHOLDERS?

Stakeholders can include investors, employees, partners, customers—anyone who has a "vested interest" in the challenge you face. They can play small or large roles in crafting the solution, in funding the project, and in influencing others to contribute. Or, they may play no role at all in implementation but have a strong interest in the outcomes. There are many different types of stakeholders, including the following:

- *Sponsors.* These are stakeholders who have presented the challenge or project and support the overall goals of the project.
- *Customers.* These stakeholders receive some benefit or end result of the project; they are directly affected by the change. They are more integrated in the process, helping guide the outcome. They may work in the company or outside of the company.
- *Implementers.* These stakeholders help get the work done, are actively engaged in producing the end result, and can control access to resources.
- *Opinion shapers.* These stakeholders are recognized opinion leaders who can provide positive or negative opinions on the project. They may act as formal or informal leaders.
- *Others.* Any person who might provide information needed by the implementers, or provide the means of getting to the solu-

tion, is considered a stakeholder. Think of the computer expert who helps create a program needed to get the project done—he or she provides a specific service for a set purpose, but isn't involved in the project day-to-day. Competitors also may be in this category. Are you implementing a change that will affect the competition in some way, such as a new product or pricing change?

USING THE STAKEHOLDER MAP

Consider a challenge for which you have to deliver results. Who are all the groups, departments, and individuals who have a stake in the challenge and should be included? Are there external groups who should be considered in the development of the solution? Which of the groups will be involved more, and who will be affected?

One tool that can assist you in answering those questions is the *stakeholder map*. By creating a visual map of your stakeholders, you can begin to better understand how the different groups connect to each other, to the project at hand, and in their relationship with you. The map will help give you a clearer picture of the primary and secondary groups you will need to include in reaching a solution.

Using Figure 2.1 as a sample, fill in your stakeholder map. Start by placing the definition of your challenge in the center, and then begin to identify the groups or individuals who you believe will play a role in the successful implementation of your challenge. Some primary stakeholders will immediately come to mind. *Place those you consider critical to the project closest to the center.* Next, begin to think about secondary groups who may not play as direct a role in implementing a solution to the challenge, but who still may be influential to its success or be affected by the changes that occur as a result. These groups will be placed farther away from the center of the challenge.

Put as many "arms" on the map as you have stakeholders. It's better to include more stakeholders at this early point to ensure you've thought through the process and the impact of the change on the internal and external stakeholders. Make sure to include anyone who may be indirectly affected or involved, but who is still influential to your challenge.

FIGURE 2.1 Blank Stakeholder Map

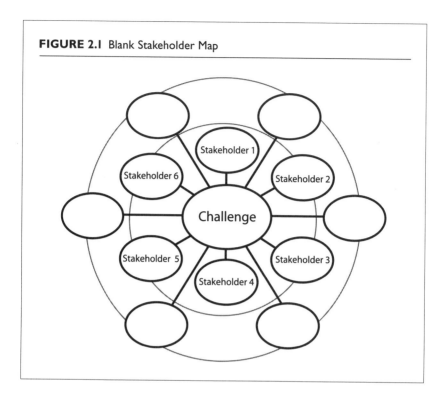

HOW THE STAKEHOLDER MAP WORKS

Another way to think about the role of the manager is to compare it with that of a host creating an invitation to a major event, for
example, a White House state dinner. Taking a look at how such a
high profile event is organized, we can begin to see how the stakeholder map might help in creating the right mix of groups. State din-
ners include a diverse mix of guests from across the world—elected
officials, cabinet members, community leaders, academics, civic
leaders, and celebrities. The occasions are very carefully planned
and orchestrated, because the eyes of the world are watching for any
slipups or subtle snubs in protocol or respect. Consider a state dinner hosted by President and Mrs. Clinton in 1997 to honor President
Jiang Zemin of China. A sample stakeholder map for the event is presented in Figure 2.2, which included the following key stakeholders:

- President and Mrs. Clinton
- President Jiang Zemin

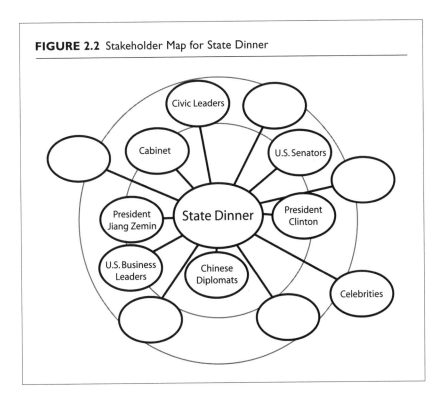

FIGURE 2.2 Stakeholder Map for State Dinner

- Prominent members of the Clinton Cabinet
- U.S. Senators
- Chinese Diplomats
- U.S. Business Leaders
- Civic Leaders
- Celebrities

Have any key groups been omitted? Now's the time to thoroughly consider all of the groups and include them from the beginning; otherwise, you could be creating monumental problems for yourself down the road. Project failure isn't necessarily due to organized resistance by stakeholders—they may simply find that the solution doesn't meet their needs and not use it as a result. Stories of corporate projects that have failed because those in charge were unable to adequately identify, assess, or communicate with one or more stakeholder groups are plentiful. How many initiatives can you cite that simply went away quietly when they didn't meet the needs of the organization?

Research has shown correlations between a team's successful performance and their level of engagement in external activities, such as stakeholder mapping, seeking feedback, coordinating, negotiating, and opening up communication channels. (Ancona, 1992)

In the state dinner example, one key group was omitted—scholars. As noted in a *New York Times* opinion piece by Stephen R. Graubard, the China scholars—active in the nation's academic institutions, research organizations, and law firms—were conspicuously absent from the event. Graubard noted that it probably wasn't that those who were omitted were particularly upset at having been left out—they, in fact, had an opportunity to meet President Jiang Zemin at another event. It was simply that a state occasion would have been an opportunity to demonstrate the depth of our intellectual engagement with China—its arts, history, achievement, and traditions—and send a strong signal that we value the scholarship we have fostered and supported.

The implications of being included can be as significant as the implications of being left out. Consider a 2005 G7 finance ministers' dinner and meeting in Britain. Prime Minister Tony Blair, host of the event, invited members of the G7 countries (the United States, Canada, Japan, France, Germany, Italy, and Britain) per usual, but also included India, Brazil, and South Africa for the first time, and China for the second time. By extending the invitation to other countries, the G7 provided a nod to these countries' rising importance in global trade, a major issue for the group. For this particular meeting, the G7 countries planned to put pressure on China for its trade practices, a pressure that China would likely tolerate, as the invitation to the dinner and talks gives the country rare access to other G7 discussions. (Maddox, February 2005)

When there is more at stake than social snubs, not having the right people at the table can be detrimental to the results that were originally envisioned—especially if conflict already exists. The newspapers report almost daily accounts of negotiations, meetings, or talks organized to bring conflicting factions together in an effort to try and peacefully resolve their differences. They run the gamut from striking union workers and business owners battling over benefits and compensation to entire nations battling over disputed ownership to land and resources. In some cases, the individuals or groups involved are so distrusting of one another or the relations are so strained that mediators are in attendance specifically to play the role of host, ensuring that everyone is treated fairly and according to established rules.

Of course these examples are extreme and the challenges historically complex. But we can learn from their experiences in approaching our own business challenges. In many cases, these groups have been unable to make progress, some for years, because key parties' interests have not been adequately represented at the table. Even when someone is an "official" spokesperson, that doesn't mean you can be sure they adequately represent the interests of all others like them. That's why you need to carefully consider who needs to be "at the table."

By understanding "who" and "why" a group is involved, you will be able to begin to identify the individuals with whom you need to build relationships to jointly craft a solution. As manager, your role is not to provide the solution; rather, it's to create the infrastructure of relationships that will lead to the best solution.

Remember that these stakeholders aren't bound by the corporate campus—consider everyone touched by a project. In the state dinner example, stakeholders are not just those who are invited to the event, but everyone who is concerned with the outcome of the visit. This may include business leaders hoping to gain access to China, Chinese diplomats, or diplomats from other countries, such as Taiwan.

Your goal is not to begin the relationship by trying to influence stakeholders; rather, it's to learn from them and include them in your solution. Stakeholders can be valuable resources for the following reasons:

- They may have faced a similar challenge in the past during another task or while working elsewhere.
- They may be able to provide a historical context to the situation, explaining some of the connections between other stakeholders and why things are the way they are.
- They may control key resources that will be critical to the success of your task.
- They may be able to use some of their existing relationships to help engage others in the challenge.

FIGURE 2.3 Olympic Bid Stakeholder Map

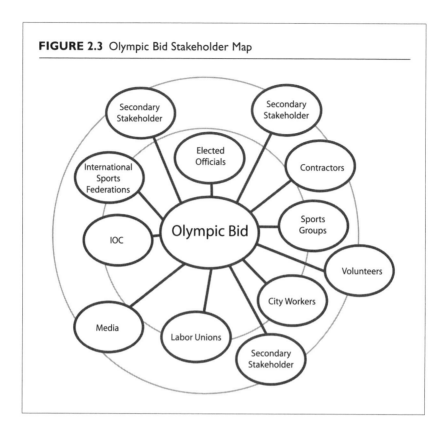

As such, their input is going to improve the quality of the solution. Using a sports example, any organizer in charge of bringing a big event to a city has to work with a number of different stakeholders. Using the Olympics as a model, if you wanted your city to host the Olympics, what stakeholders would you need to contact initially to get the ball rolling?

As shown in Figure 2.3, the following stakeholders should be considered:

- *Elected officials.* You need the backing of elected officials because you will face challenges that only they can push through, such as major state funding for construction of venues. Local elected officials, such as the mayor, city council, local congressional delegation, county officials, and others, will play a major role in helping put the pieces together.

- *Sports groups.* This group of stakeholders is important to you because without their buy-in and help, your chances of being taken seriously by the International Olympic Committee members are jeopardized. Gaining both the endorsement of key sports leaders and their input on what size and type of venue they need for their sport will be crucial to success. Also consider how this group can lead you to other key stakeholders as you move forward in the process—you'll be adding stakeholders along the way.
- *International sports federations.* Keeping the international groups in the loop will help build your credibility. Although initially this group may not be a key player, the group will become more important down the line and should be considered part of the initial stakeholder map.
- *International Olympic Committee.* This is the group you are working to convince. They are stakeholders as well because of their experience and knowledge of the process.
- *Labor unions or city workers.* This group of stakeholders could be considered the "worker bees" of the effort. Included here are Department of Transportation workers to help with moving people along roads and at airports, bus stations, and train stops; city sanitation workers to keep venues and the city clean during the 18-day event; the city water and sewer department to handle additional demand; and other similar workers.
- *Contractors.* Can local contractors do the work necessary to get all of the venues you need up and running by the due date? This group of stakeholders is critical to your success—the event as a whole could fail if even one venue is not completed by the time the Olympic Games take place.
- *Media.* Because the media acts as a portal of information for the general public, this group of stakeholders needs to be included to a certain extent to carry your message and vision to the people.
- *Volunteers.* For an event of this size, you need to be sure the local volunteer community can be mobilized to fill the many positions required. Will there be enough people interested in this type of event to make it happen?

FIGURE 2.4 "Relativity"

THE MANAGER'S CHALLENGE

Take a look at the image in Figure 2.4, "Relativity" by M.C. Escher. The "measured chaos" in the drawing shows each person in his own world and dimension moving through a common space, but each is on a different level, going in a different direction, and has a different reality. The image is effective in illustrating the difficult challenge a manager faces in bringing people with different perspectives and different goals together.

This is the essence of what you, the manager, must do. Your job is to draw this disparate group toward a common position in order to solve a problem or craft change. Leading each of your stakeholders from their unique positions to this common alignment or position can be greatly enhanced through the development of relationships with each person involved.

Once you begin exploring all of the "staircases" across the organization—how they connect and where they lead—you will be able to better identify more and more stakeholders, and potentially more widespread implications of particular solutions. There are also many doors that lead to new areas or lead outside the confines of this structure to stakeholders in other worlds.

BUILDING YOUR STAKEHOLDER MAP

Identifying your stakeholders is the first step toward crafting the best, most sustaining solutions for change. By thinking about whom your stakeholders are and what their roles and interests are, you will begin to find the right road to a shared solution.

CHECKLIST

- ❑ Place your challenge at the center of a stakeholder map.
- ❑ Fill in the initial primary stakeholders that come to mind.
- ❑ Ask some exploratory questions to help identify additional stakeholders.
  - Who controls the necessary financial or staffing resources?
  - Who will benefit from the proposed solution? Who will not?
  - What external stakeholders will be affected by or have an interest in the challenge, such as vendors, partners, or even competitors?

CHAPTER THREE

THINK RELATIONSHIPS, NOT TRANSACTIONS

IN THIS CHAPTER

Reviewing Your Stakeholder Relationships ■ Relationships Need Nurturing ■ Opportunities to Connect ■ Effective Communication Skills ■ Building Your Stakeholder Relationships

As a manager, you ultimately are responsible for driving solutions and making things happen in your organization. You won't be able to develop and implement solutions single-handedly. You have to be able to get information from, collaborate with, and influence stakeholders across your network. Thus, to design the best solutions, you have to begin forming productive, sustainable relationships with these stakeholders early in the process.

Now that you have identified some of the departments, groups, or individuals who will play a role, directly or indirectly, in developing the best solution to your challenge, think about the existing relationships you have with each member and the relationships you must begin building. Although you may be anxious to get started and begin making progress on the various projects you've been assigned, you need to connect with and learn more about both the stakeholders involved and the workings of the organization. Now is the time to make connections with stakeholders who you don't know well, or to strengthen your existing relationships.

FIGURE 3.1 Stakeholder Relationship Map

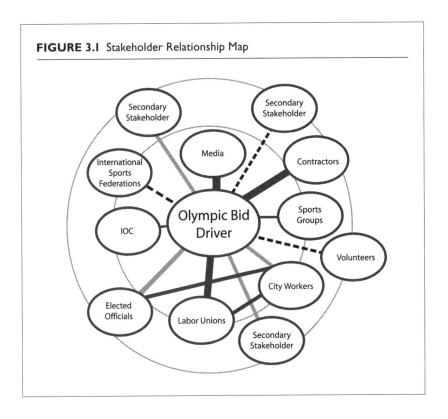

REVIEWING YOUR
STAKEHOLDER RELATIONSHIPS

Let's look at the Olympic Bid stakeholder map from Chapter 2 from a different perspective. If we now place the Olympic Bid Driver at the center of this map, rather than the challenge itself, consider the types of relationships and connections that exist with and between the surrounding stakeholders. In Figure 3.1 we see the strength of relationships represented by a variety of lines connecting them to the Bid Driver. The strongest relationships are indicated by a heavy, bold connection line. Other relationships—weak but amicable, strained due to previous problems, or those missing altogether—are represented by thinner, grayer, or dotted connections.

Why are these relationships important? Because you can't implement alone. You need to involve others, get their input and support, and collaborate well as you move forward. People are more likely to cooperate with someone they know and with whom they have a connection. Also, you never can know fully who might have an idea, resource, or vote of confidence you'll need. For these reasons, among others, you need to connect to a wide range of stakeholders, both for a specific project and to be effective in general.

You have a head start, though. With the general shift in the workplace from top-down management to integrated work processes, it is likely that you already are working across various organizational boundaries and with a variety of people. Then, with the larger number of partnerships and joint ventures companies are engaged in today, the number of external stakeholders you interact with is growing. You are already beginning to keep good company, but you could do more.

Your workplace is dynamic. New players are entering the field on a regular basis. Do you find yourself occasionally looking around your own office and seeing a number of unfamiliar faces? Now think of all those you can't see directly—there are many others joining other divisions, sitting in other buildings and in remote offices that you don't see. Who are they? What do they do? What are their backgrounds and strengths? Chances are they are some of your new stakeholders and you need to make an effort to begin connecting with them.

External stakeholders are just as dynamic. There are new suppliers, customers, and partners. Think about the variety of external stakeholders with whom you interact today. Their staffs also are likely growing and changing. It may be apparent to you by now that the stakeholder map you outlined in the previous chapter should be done in pencil, because there will be quite a few edits as you go forward.

Consider the case of a university in the northern United States. The administration wanted to simplify the accounting and procurement systems used across the university. They had several systems that didn't align, making it difficult to calculate an overall operating budget, make capital investment decisions, project shortfalls, and the like. The administration decided to overhaul the financial applications, and have all departments and schools within the university shift to one common system. A small group of people in the university Information Technology office interviewed potential software vendors, getting all the details on the back-end structure, system stability and robustness, user interface, and reporting capability. The project team then selected a vendor for this multimillion-dollar project.

After the selection process came the implementation phase. At this point, the project team and administration invited representatives from all the departments and schools to meet with them and begin working with the chosen system. The departments, as the end users, needed to understand how the system worked in general, how to migrate their existing data over to the new system, and then how to use it to do their day-to-day tasks. The project team thought this would be a relatively simple process.

Unfortunately, as they began working with the department representatives, it became clear that this new, very expensive system would not meet the stakeholders' needs. It could not accommodate the range of accounting and procurement needs present in the university. For example, the reports functions didn't allow researchers to track expenses against specific grants. Some schools needed to budget for graduate student stipends, and there was no line item for those costs. The team wasn't aware of any of these (and other) requirements when they met with potential vendors.

The project team hadn't consulted with the end users on how they would use the system, either. The accounting system that they chose had been adapted from one designed for a manufacturing company. The menu organization and navigation were counterintuitive; line items that should be, in an academic setting, grouped together, were located several menus apart. The names for commands were unfamiliar. The department secretaries found the interface difficult to use and were frustrated that the new system would make their jobs much harder.

In all, because the team had waited too long to involve critical stakeholders, they selected a system that didn't meet the university's needs. They committed to spend five years of technology budget only to discover afterwards that the system would never be implemented because it didn't meet the end users' needs.

Had the project team met up front with the department representatives, they could have discovered the range of tasks the separate systems handled and found out what features were essential for the end users. They could have tested different interfaces with a representative sample and determined earlier what the problems would be. By not connecting with the stakeholders early on, they bought the wrong product and created ill will among those who would implement the system.

RELATIONSHIPS NEED NURTURING

Relationships don't happen overnight, they take time. Because they take time, thought, and effort to develop, some managers dismiss the importance of relationship building. When up against tasks that are more urgent and immediate, taking time to work on stakeholder relationships is a low priority. However, by the time you need to make something happen, it could be too late. Without expending the energy to connect with key stakeholders on a personal level, a manager risks losing effectiveness down the road.

Think about it this way: Suppose a new manager enters the workplace and neglects to build relationships with coworkers, colleagues, and others—"I'm here to work, not socialize!" He keeps his head down, finishes his daily routine without incident, and goes home. However, when a new project comes up or an unusual problem erupts, he may not know who to talk to or won't know who might help him—he doesn't *have* any relationships. He has to resort to the old, detached way of management—using formal channels to get information and issue requests—without a clue whether colleagues, coworkers, customers, or other stakeholders will go along with his directives, or if they have knowledge and expertise that could have helped had he only known who to ask.

People need social capital to get work done. When a need arises, people are much more forthcoming with additional information, willing to collaborate on special projects, or give the extra effort needed to solve complex issues when a request comes from someone with whom they have a previous connection.

Take, for example, Elena, who works in a popular division of a large-sized company. As a human resources (HR) professional, she is constantly being asked to fill out surveys and provide data for benchmarking. How does Elena choose where to spend her time—which ones to ignore or delete and which to reply to? Simple. If it's a request from someone she knows and likes, she'll fill it out. She may also decide to help if it's from an organization she respects, and she wants access to what they find (many surveys will share the summarized data with those who contributed, but not with others). Requests and surveys from any other source go unanswered.

Remember, relationships go in both directions. As you are making connections with people, they are making connections with you.

OPPORTUNITIES TO CONNECT

Riding in the elevator, premeeting small talk, company gatherings—all of these can be prime opportunities to meet people and make connections. Managers sometimes opt not to attend optional events, thinking it's much more valuable to keep working on whatever important project is at hand. Start taking advantage of these opportunities to connect to stakeholders. Rather than interacting with the "regulars" with whom you already have relationships, seek out the new people around the meeting table or in the lunchroom.

"Hi. I'm new around here."

© The New Yorker Collection, 1993. Jack Ziegler, from cartoonbank.com. All Rights Reserved.

Create Your Own Opportunities

Taking advantage of opportunities that present themselves naturally is a good approach but will only take you so far. Consider how to create opportunities to interact with stakeholders, especially those not located in your office. Following are some examples:

- When appropriate, invite clients or vendors to attend company functions. They, too, might welcome opportunities to interact. Just make sure you introduce them to everyone else!
- Host an occasional open invitation "brown bag lunch" session to chat about new initiatives or to demonstrate new technologies within your area.
- Use the strong relationships that you have already established to help make connections between other stakeholders.
- Visit colleagues at the company's other locations and offices.
- Join professional organizations or find conferences to attend. Meet others in your industry or field.
- Seek out and attend vendor events.

First Impressions Count

Have you ever been on or heard stories of really bad first dates? The guy with the really bad breath, the woman who wore too much makeup, the person who spent the entire night telling stories of relationships past . . . ? Have you interviewed a job candidate who chewed gum loudly, and asked how he could get your job? Consider another candidate who was well informed about the company, neatly groomed, and prepared with insightful questions to ask. Every new situation has a "first impression" moment. How you look, how you speak, how you walk, your attitude—the people you meet assess all of these factors and many more instantly, and that assessment is both conscious and unconscious. When it comes to creating a positive first impression, self-awareness can make the difference.

Although it's easy to dispute the topic of first impressions because it leans heavily toward superficial orientations, it is a powerful perception that should not be dismissed. Based on prior research of nonverbal behavior and physical attractiveness, it's estimated that visual assessment takes less than ten seconds and a verbal assessment less than two minutes. These studies have shown that assessments are not only done quickly, they are lasting. Knowing that first impressions are formed quickly, it is important to remain cognizant of your personal presence. It's not about looks or charm; it's about knowing how to optimize those ten-second chances at winning a positive first impression. (Ambady and Rosenthal, 1993)

When it comes to first impressions, preparation is essential. Make sure you do your homework before you begin to talk with your stakeholders. Are there common interests or connections between you and your stakeholder? What can you do to ally yourself with him or her in those first two minutes of conversation? You can ensure an immediate connection by asking good questions and demonstrating interest. Doing the legwork prior to your interaction will demonstrate that you have a sincere wish to build a relationship and open the door to more meaningful conversations. Before you meet with each stakeholder, you should be able to answer the following questions:

- What role or function do they have within the organization?
- What are their biggest concerns?
- What information will they want from you?

Don't forget that it's not all about you. People will immediately disengage if they detect you are not interacting with sincere interest. Go into each interaction with the mind-set of an anthropologist. Your main goal is to find out as much as you can about the individual to get insights on how to best relate to him or her. Approaching each interaction with curiosity and inquiry will open the door for your stakeholders to engage with you in a manner that ultimately builds the trust you need to sustain the relationship in the future.

EFFECTIVE COMMUNICATION SKILLS

If you haven't developed good communication skills, now is the time to concentrate on doing so. An effective communication style will enhance your ability to make a good first impression and to build strong relationships.

Effective communication is also more than what you *say*. John Gottman, professor of psychology at the University of Washington, has done extensive research on predictors of marital stability and divorce based on observing couples' emotions, physiology (such as changes in heart rate), facial expressions, and communication patterns as they discuss a major topic of disagreement. Interestingly, his research found that when one of the partners withdrew as a listener—less eye contact, fewer facial expressions, and fewer nonverbal responses, such as nodding—marital satisfaction was more likely to decrease over time. (Gottman, 2001)

Going back to our influence process, "first conversations" with stakeholders should be approached without any goal in mind, other than building rapport and learning more about their interests and concerns.

- *Become an "active listener."* Ask questions. Check that you understand the other's point. Be conscious of balancing airtime, and balancing the focus; what is the right mix of asking questions and asserting your position on issues? If you're doing all the talking, you're not in a conversation—you're lecturing "one-on-one." Let go of any specific agenda, other than to learn more about this particular stakeholder.
- *Don't interrogate.* Conversations should have give and take. Both parties listen, ask questions, and reveal information. You aren't interrogating the person, so be conscious of how you frame questions and provide information about yourself as well.
- *Express sincere interest in what the other person is saying.* People talk about what is most important to them, and this is what you are seeking out. Some of these topics, even if they seem a bit of a waste of time at the moment, give you a "prompt" for opening other conversations later on, when you may need the support of this stakeholder.
- *Maintain good eye contact.* In western cultures, eye contact is usually an important indicator of focus and interest. Remember the power that eye contact can have—candidates for public office have proven that this is a powerful tool to use in connecting with constituents. Contrast the politician who shakes someone's hand while looking the constituent in his eyes and truly making that connection with the one who grasps one hand while looking down the line at the next person. You can imagine which of the two makes the better impression. Keep in mind that direct eye contact can be considered rude or disrespectful by other cultures, such as some Asian or Native American cultures. Be attentive to the preferences of your stakeholders.

- *Be conscious of body language.* Body language can tell you volumes about what the other person is *really* saying. There are many different types of nonverbal communication: facial expressions, the clues in our voices, hand gestures, body movements, touch, and personal space. Every culture has its own unwritten rules regarding nonverbal communications. For example, in some cultures, the classic "closed" person has arms crossed, legs crossed (when sitting), and a stern or blank expression on his or her face. Approach this person as openly as possible and see what impact your confident walk, smiling face, outstretched hand, and positive leading question will have.

As the relationship develops, more information can be shared and learned. Remember that relationship building is ongoing—you don't know when you'll need to engage a particular stakeholder in a project, so you need to maintain relationships throughout your career.

BUILDING YOUR STAKEHOLDER RELATIONSHIPS

What you learn about people is a work in progress, similar to the way solutions to problems will be developed along the way. The informal day-to-day opportunities for interaction are as important as the official meetings and conferences. The relationships you build should be dynamic and ever evolving. There's no end to these relationships—they keep growing and changing, adjusting along the way.

CHECKLIST

❑ Map your current stakeholder relationships.
  - Consider where you or your team needs to build, repair, or strengthen relationships.
❑ Plan, create, and take advantage of opportunities to interact.
  - Don't forget first impression do's and don'ts.
  - Brush up on communication skills—speaking and listening.
❑ Keep going—relationships are built over time.

CHAPTER FOUR

TAKING THE TEMPERATURE

IN THIS CHAPTER

A Baseline Temperature ■ Connecting Work and
People ■ Stakeholder Analysis ■ Where Can It Go Wrong?
■ Building Your Stakeholder Analysis

Now that you have identified the groups and individuals involved in your challenge—the sponsors, customers, collaborators, in-
fluencers, and others—you need to assess how much you currently
know about them and what you still need to discover.

A BASELINE TEMPERATURE

You need to "take the temperature" of each stakeholder group as
a baseline from which to move forward. In other words, check the
water before diving in. It may be your inclination to delve right into
a project, but that could be a mistake because you don't have all the
information you need to make decisions. In thinking about your
stakeholders, consider both how they connect to work that needs to
be done as part of your challenge, and how your relationships with
them can help increase your ability to build a better solution and influence results. There is likely a variety of work connections and people connections that need to be developed or strengthened.

One of the largest "parties" ever hosted is the Olympic Games. Host cities go through an extensive selection process and spend years planning for and coordinating the event. The list of primary stakeholders—all of the participating athletes, trainers, officials, and host city service workers—seems endless. Include the tens of millions of people who will follow the events on television or in the newspapers and that number becomes mind boggling.

Let's consider the process involved in generating Atlanta's bid to host the Olympic Games in 1996. In February 1987, Billy Payne, a successful Atlanta attorney, decided that he wanted to bring the 1996 Olympic Games to Atlanta. Other cities had been involved in the bid process for a long time—the United States Olympic Committee (USOC) planned to make a decision in April 1988. Payne had to quickly develop a team and a strategy.

His first challenge: to secure Atlanta as the USOC's submission to the International Olympic Committee's competition for the 1996 Olympic Games. If Payne had used a stakeholder map to chart the process to achieving his goal, he would have started out with the challenge—beating other cities for the sole submission by the USOC—at the center of the map. Next, he would have started to consider his stakeholders.

Working with his friends, Payne was able to identify the stakeholders he needed to get the process started. By group, he knew he needed to work with Atlanta corporations, elected officials, and civic leaders; he also knew he needed expertise in research, fundraising, and project management. Some relationships had to be enhanced, others started from scratch. By identifying which groups he needed, he was able to move forward with the goal in mind.

Next, Payne started to consider his own network, and who might have connections to these stakeholder groups.

- Who could lobby Atlanta's civic leaders and key politicians?
- Who could gain buy-in from corporations?
- What relationships were already in place?
- What relationships needed to be developed?
- Who could provide research and information on how cities bid for the Olympics?
- Who would help him prepare the bid submission?
- Who would finance the operation?

Payne began making phone calls. One friend in particular, Peter Candler, put Payne in touch with the people who would become his core group. Candler connected Payne with Horace Sibley, a partner in the prestigious law firm King and Spalding. Sibley had powerful connections with corporations and elected officials and could handle that domain. Candler also introduced Payne to Ginger Watkins, who had extensive experience with fundraising and volunteer work and who also provided another layer of social connections. She became the research arm of the group. For financing, each member of the core group contributed an average of $50,000 to cover costs of the professional proposal they had to prepare.

As the deadline for a decision from the USOC approached, Payne brought in more local leaders to help influence the USOC board and create a compelling invitation. Keeping the challenge in mind, Payne and his stakeholders embarked on a plan to "divide and conquer" the 100+ members of the USOC board. The stakeholders called members, invited them to visit the stakeholders in their hometowns, and invited them to visit Atlanta. In April 1988, the Atlanta Committee for the Olympic Games "one-upped" Minneapolis, the only other competitor for the USOC's bid, by hosting a lavish reception in Washington, which was well-attended by Atlanta dignitaries, including Mayor Andrew Young, and sports celebrities.

Payne and his stakeholders achieved their goal—they were chosen to be the host city submitted by the U.S. Olympic Committee for consideration by the International Olympic Committee. Through careful mapping of the goal and what relationships would be needed to achieve the goal, the group was successful in achieving this first step on the road to the 1996 Summer Games.

CONNECTING WORK AND PEOPLE

What do you now know about your challenge and the stakeholders who have a connection to it? Consider the following:

Connecting the Work

- What do you know about your stakeholders' functions and day-to-day work within their department or group?

- What do you know about their special interests and how they relate to your challenge?
- Do you know anything about their likely level of support for the project?
- How critical is their support and participation to your success?
- What capacity do they have to participate?
- At what stages of the project will their participation and support be most valuable?

Connecting the People

- What do you know about the individuals you've identified?
- What are their areas of expertise?
- How influential will they be with other stakeholders or people outside the organization?
- What do you know about any conflicts of interest between stakeholders?
- Which stakeholders do you need to develop alliances with?
- Are you aware of any existing relationships between stakeholders that you can use to help build alliances?
- Have they participated in any early conversations about the challenge you have?
- Where are there gaps in your relationships and connections across the network?
- Where are there strong connections and alliances?

STAKEHOLDER ANALYSIS

Using a *stakeholder analysis* chart, like the one in Figure 4.1, can help you work through this phase of the process. Begin by assessing what you know now about whom the stakeholders are, their current level of support for or resistance to your challenge, the level of support that you aspire to have, and their particular issues of interest.

Stakeholder. List the stakeholder groups that you have identified, as well as personal contacts that you have or need to make within each group.

FIGURE 4.1 Stakeholder Analysis Chart

Stakeholder	Desired Support Level	Current Support Level	Open Issues: Interests and Concerns

Level of support. Based on what you currently know about this stakeholder group or individual, estimate both their current level of support and the level of support that you would like to achieve. Desired support level may be driven by multiple factors: the amount of influence they have with other stakeholders, the resources that they control, or the amount of direct involvement that they will have with the project. Five types of support levels are listed below.

1. *Active supporter = Score 2.* This person already may have pledged to provide the time, people, and personal credibility to support the project.
2. *Passive supporter = Score 1.* This person is in agreement that the project should be done, but may not play an active role in making it happen.
3. *Neutral = Score 0.* This person has no strong opinions about the project.
4. *Passive resistor = Score –1.* This person is against the project but unlikely to take any action.
5. *Active resistor = Score –2.* This person is strongly against the project and will likely take action or vocally resist the project.

Open issues. Within the Open Issues column, list all interests or concerns to note with this stakeholder. This column should explain why you gave each stakeholder the rating level you did. Review the lists of questions connecting the work and people at the beginning of this chapter. Can you answer these questions? Make a note of both what you know and what you need to learn. Were you able to assess the desired support and current support levels? How confident are you of these scores? If you find that you had trouble gauging their support level, this is also an indicator that you need to learn more about this stakeholder and should be noted.

What have you accomplished with this activity? First, you've identified the key individuals who will be affected directly or indirectly, positively or negatively, by the challenge.

Second, you have clarified where you need to build or strengthen existing relationships. If you are new to the company or division, this may seem the most daunting task—there may be many people with whom you need to build relationships, not just improve relationships. The stakeholder analysis will help you prioritize your conversations. It will keep you "on task" and focused on improving the buy-in.

Third, you have charted where the stakeholders are now in comparison to where you need them to be. Now you have to come up with a plan to develop your relationship with each stakeholder, learn more about his or her positions, and influence a shared solution to the challenge.

WHERE CAN IT GO WRONG?

Most of us can probably think of new initiatives or projects that had a high visibility for a while, proposed that change was coming, and then seemed to just lose momentum. Sometimes work on the challenge ends because of a new strategic direction, other times a solution was actually crafted that never catches on with stakeholders. What went wrong?

Sometimes people forget to contact a stakeholder or contact a stakeholder late in the process. In other cases, they may miss the mark in their assessments and someone they thought was a strong supporter turns out to actively block their efforts. Sometimes they don't get active resistance from any stakeholders, but the solution turns out to be less than optimum because they didn't engage the stakeholder in a manner that connected with them and encouraged them to provide input.

One special projects director relates: "I was asked to lead a project team in selecting and installing a CRM system for our sales force. I went through the motions of contacting different stakeholders, inviting them to open sessions, and getting their feedback. But the truth is I didn't really think I was going to learn anything useful from them. They seemed too busy in their own work to give much thought about our project, and besides, I thought our group knew best what they needed. In our sessions, we spent more time presenting than we did really asking questions and trying to learn about their needs. Our real goal was to check their names off as having been included so that no one could later complain that they were not consulted. No one *actively* resisted, and the system was purchased and installed. Now we have an expensive piece of software that no one actually uses. Although technically we delivered what we were supposed to, it wasn't a valuable or sustainable solution for the company—and the sales force is still struggling with the same issues it had originally."

In a larger-scale example, both Coca-Cola and Pepsi may have missed the mark with their mid-calorie colas introduced during 2004. With half the sugar and carbohydrates of regular colas, the rival products are aimed largely at diet-conscious consumers who don't like the taste of artificial sweeteners. The companies also hoped to benefit from the "low carb craze" that was sweeping the nation. Despite huge marketing campaigns for both products, the new colas did not perform as well as the companies had hoped. Perhaps Coke and Pepsi had misgauged their key stakeholders' behavior: Anyone on a diet is more likely to reach for a zero-calorie soft drink than a 70-calorie soft drink. And, the sugar and carbohydrate numbers in the soft drinks were still too high for some diet programs, such as Atkins. (MacArthur, 2004)

By not taking into consideration the behaviors of their key stakeholders—their diet-conscious consumers—both companies were unable to create a new product niche. This illustrates the need for fully understanding *all* stakeholders involved in new product launches, new strategies, or new ideas. You've got to know everything possible about your stakeholders to bring about change.

BUILDING YOUR STAKEHOLDER ANALYSIS

A thorough assessment of your stakeholders will arm you with vital information needed to make decisions and create solutions. By using this tool, you will learn more about your colleagues, their strengths and weaknesses, and how they can help in the process of crafting change. The analysis will also show you where you need to put additional energy toward building relationships. It's a powerful tool.

CHECKLIST

❏ Create a stakeholder analysis chart for the stakeholders you have identified.

❏ Consider the *Connections to Work* and *Connections to People* guiding questions.

- Are there gaps in your relationships with stakeholders?
- Are there places where their support levels are lower than desired?
- What issues must be addressed as you proceed?
- Based on what you know right now about your stakeholders, who should contact each stakeholder—you or someone else from your project team or network?

❏ Where could things go wrong? Identify the weak spots.

WHAT'S YOUR STORY?

Take a step back and reflect on the panoramic view of both your challenge and your stakeholders. You have identified most of the stakeholders who will play a role in the challenge you are facing and have completed an initial assessment of the nature of their connections to the work at hand and to the people involved. You have some preliminary ideas about what parts of the challenge stakeholders are most likely to be concerned about, where they will need to know more, and where their experience and knowledge is going to be invaluable. Now what?

Your own vision for the future and a plan in tow do not necessarily prime you for effective execution. You need to be able to communicate your plan to others in a way that will make it personal for them and, as a result, inspire them to action. You may be excited and challenged by the task at hand and the possibilities that exist, but you will need more than a bulleted list of facts and figures to engage others. One approach to communicating your message in a compelling way is through storytelling.

STORYTELLING
A Timeless Method

Why tell stories? In the words of playwright Jean Anouilh: "Fiction gives life its form." In its most elemental form, stories encapsulate human experience and serve as one of the most powerful forms of human communication. Creating a narrative is a basic human instinct. Think of the backdrops against which stories have set the stage: history, religion, politics, philosophy, the arts. We tell stories as a way to make sense of the world around us, as a way to infuse structure and meaning in our daily lives, and as a way to connect our life experiences to others.

A "good story" is the key element and it is what we are seeking in the books we read, the movies we watch, or the poetry or music that we listen to. A good story, be it in book, film, or song, is so engaging that we can recite entire segments of dialogue or keep reviewing dramatic scenes in our head. The message sticks with us long after the story has ended. While we may forget other details about when it was created, who the writer was, or what actor played a certain character, the stories we tend to remember.

Research has corroborated the effectiveness of stories. Organizational sociologists Joanne Martin and Melanie Powers compared the use of four different persuasion methods in an attempt to convince MBA students that a particular company had actually practiced their stated policy of avoiding layoffs. Groups of students were presented with statistics only, statistics and a story, a story only, or an official policy statement made by a company executive. The results: Only 5 percent to 10 percent of the students were persuaded by statistics alone; those who were told only a story believed the company's claims more often (65% to 75%) than the other three groups. (Martin and Powers, 1982)

The use of storytelling has been recognized as a valuable business tool. One of the leaders in the field, Robert McKee, has perfected the art of storytelling. McKee has had a long career in the entertainment industry as an actor, director, playwright, screenwriter, and popular writing consultant. His best-selling book, *Story* (Regan Books/HarperCollins), is often required reading for film and cinema students at top universities across the country. His hugely popular weekend "Story Seminar" has had more than 40,000 attend-ees, including many creative staff members sent by their firms to learn more about the art of crafting a good story. McKee is also a project consultant to major corporations—he believes that executives can better reach their goals if they learn to engage the emotions of their people, rather than focusing on rhetoric, statistics, and facts. Even if they are somewhat persuaded by the facts and figures, it is only on an intellectual level. Their hearts aren't engaged, and the key to their hearts is a good story. Just like a good movie or book, we will tend to forget the bulleted lists and the data from a presentation, but the stories we remember. (McKee, 2003)

A POWERFUL INFLUENCING APPROACH

Why tell stories as a tool for influence? Allan Kay, well known for his work in developing and advancing early personal computing technologies and now president of Viewpoints Research Institute, Inc., has been quoted often as saying: "Why was Solomon recog-nized as the wisest man in the world? Because he knew more stories (proverbs) than anyone else. Scratch the surface in a typical board-room and we're all just cavemen with briefcases, hungry for a wise person to tell us stories."

The plight of human existence is not a common topic in most boardroom meetings; however, it's important to realize that human connection is something we all seek. In an environment where facts are the basis for most decisions, telling stories in the workplace can serve as a powerful means to influence strategy. As a leader, using storytelling as a form of communication can help you create authen-tic and meaningful relationships while mobilizing your colleagues around your vision for the work at hand.

Storytelling is as much about the teller as it is about the listener. Your fundamental goal is to create alignment and action around your challenge. To do so, you must communicate in a way that not only engages your audience but also includes them in the picture as an integral part of the solution. Crafting a simple, compelling message will help you set the context for the work that needs to be done. In using this message, and by appealing to your stakeholders through

The storytelling method has found a niche in the medical field. Dr. Rita Charon, professor of internal medicine at New York City's Columbia University, initiated their Program in Narrative Medicine as a way to shift students' focus toward the whole patient experience. She sees the patient's hospital chart—filled with notes from the various people involved in the care-giving process—as a novel, but missing key information about the patient's story, such as fears, expectations, disappointments, and pain. As part of this program, future doctors keep parallel charts. Besides the traditional charts with information largely undecipherable to the rest of us, they also write about their encounters with patients in ordinary language. They track not just the patients' physical symptoms and ailments but her entire hospital experience. The result is a shared narrative of stories about their patients' experiences intermixed with their own stories of providing treatment.

Students then meet once a week to read what they have written in small group sessions. As they tell their stories to one another, the focus is not on the scientific information found in the traditional charts, but on the drama of their experiences. The methodology was deemed as beneficial by 82 percent of the participating students, both as an outlet for the pressures of residency and as a way to prepare for conversations with the patients and their families. (Pollack, 2003)

reason, emotion, and imagination, you will be engaging more than the minds of your stakeholders, resulting in a core network of individuals who will be anxious to help you develop the story further and take your message on board as their own.

To communicate your message authentically, you have to be grounded in your own story and fully understand how it relates to the context of the work and the people. You can ensure a meaningful connection by connecting to the bigger picture, reinforcing your company's values and culture, defining success, and tying your story to your audience's aspirations and needs.

As you go through the process of crafting your message, you need to consider that this is only the first phase of the process. You create a first draft of the story, and then you will need to bring others in as collaborators. You might lay out some guiding questions for yourself (or use the ones offered in this chapter) as you frame your thoughts, then use the same set with your stakeholders as you gather and incorporate their feedback. First, though, let's work through a first draft.

CRAFTING YOUR STORY AND MESSAGE

Think about the way that you may have prepared presentations in the past. Although it certainly took some time and effort to organize and refine, it wasn't terribly difficult. Business presentations intended to inform or influence the audience are largely a matter of weaving a lot of information into an allotted period of time. You may be sold on the method of storytelling, but unsure where to start or how difficult it is going to be.

As McKee notes, it takes a rational approach but not a lot of creativity to design an argument using the standard business rhetoric. It is much harder to craft a compelling story that will present your ideas with enough passion to make them memorable. Think about the best books you've read, speeches you've heard, plays you've seen. What was it about that story that captured your attention and imagination? As you begin to think about the key messages in your story, remember the essential elements of a good story. A good story

- is simple,
- is memorable,
- conveys what is important,
- stimulates dialogue, and
- evolves through an iterative process.

Crafting a compelling story around simple truths and facts allows you to strip away complexity and succinctly communicate your vision for the work ahead. Storytelling isn't being manipulative or deceptive, it is simply effective communication. If you have little of value to say, neither a polished presentation nor a story will make it more effective.

With your specific initiative or challenge in mind, you should construct your message around the basic elements of storytelling.

Set the Stage and Shape the Context

Begin with the situation or challenge and why it is important. Connect its importance to you and to your audience by focusing on interests in the challenge instead of positions to preferred solutions. If you begin with positions, people naturally think and talk about positions, rather than focusing on interests they may have in common. Instead, use the stakeholders' interests to frame issues in a way that will encourage interaction and collaboration for a creative solution.

	What is the current situation?
	What are the opportunities?
Set the Stage	Why is this initiative important to the company strategy and efforts?
	What does it mean to the work, priorities, and challenges for your team?

Introduce the Drama

Present the problem or issue that needs to be overcome so that the audience can understand it on an emotional level. What are the obstacles to overcome? What are the risks? What are the potential gains? Acknowledge the downside of the situation—where you know it will be hard—as well as the positive. Presenting only a positive spin and outcome is not believable and can damage your credibility for future influence.

Introduce the Drama	What's at risk if you don't do this?
	What are the benefits?
	What obstacles or challenges are you likely to encounter? How can you and your team overcome them?

Make It Personal

Concentrate on your stakeholders' interests and concerns and not on your own. What's in it for them? How might it affect them? How can they help? Why is this need immediate? This is where you draw them into the story so that they begin to have a connection to the challenge and also begin to see themselves as part of the solution.

Make It Personal	What does this mean for your team?
	What does this mean for others?

Inspire Action

Create a call to action. Describe the end result you envision and demonstrate how this can be a win for everyone. Describe the destination: Where are we going? What do we need to do to get there?

A **story can be** short and simple but still create a powerful call to action. The first large polio epidemic in the United States occurred in 1916 and became a more visible problem when Franklin D. Roosevelt contracted the disease in 1921. Roosevelt later built a spa in Warm Springs, Georgia, when he noticed the therapeutic effects of the warm spring waters. He also established the nonprofit Warm Springs Foundation. During the Great Depression, the foundation appealed to the general public for donations, but there was little to give.

By 1938, polio was taking a great toll on the nation, especially on infants and children. Roosevelt formed a new organization, the National Foundation for Infantile Paralysis. But funds were still sorely needed for research and to aid victims. People understood the devastating effects of contracting polio—many of them had experienced them firsthand—and they agreed that something had to be done to find a cure. But what could they do? The amount of money needed for research to find a cure was enormous and they didn't have that kind of money—they couldn't even envision that much money.

What happened next demonstrates the power of a good story. The foundation created a call to action that told the American public a compelling story about what each of them could do by contributing one dime at a time: the "March of Dimes." People all over the country were asked to send their dimes directly to the White House. The campaign proved to be hugely successful, with over $1 million contributed. This money was used to fund research by Dr. Jonas Salk, who produced the first experimental vaccine in 1948. By 1954, nationwide testing had begun. The vaccine was declared "safe, effective, and potent," and over 450 million doses would be administered over the next four years. Polio would no longer threaten public health in this country. The National Foundation would officially change its name to the March of Dimes in 1979, and go on to other visions, such as eradicating birth defects. (March of Dimes, 2004)

	What does success look like?
Inspire Action	What actions are required to get there?
	What agreements need to be made?
	How can we work together to make it happen?

Storytelling is a powerful method for getting your message across to your stakeholders. The right story is an effective tool to keep your stakeholders engaged in the project; it can be used to communicate your message in a clear, easily understood way.

CHECKLIST

- ❏ Do you have a story? Do you understand it?
- ❏ Does your story have the key elements?
  - Sets the stage
  - Introduces the drama
  - Makes it personal
  - Inspires action
- ❏ What's the key message in your story?

CHAPTER SIX

TAILORING YOUR MESSAGE AND APPROACH

IN THIS CHAPTER

Shaping the Message ■ The Elevator Version ■ Adapting to
Stakeholders' Personal Styles ■ Building a Personalized Message

Now that you know more about the various groups of stakeholders and have crafted a first version of the story you think will most engage them, consider the best approach to take with *each* stakeholder. Although the core message and goal of your story should remain consistent, you will need to tailor the message to address each stakeholder's primary concerns.

Why should you tailor your message? Doesn't that make you seem inconsistent? Tailoring your message is not about shifting your point of view or position on an issue to be more in line with whichever stakeholder you happen to be speaking with at the time. It is about adapting your delivery and emphasis to ensure that you are addressing the issues with which they are most concerned. It's about using language that is easily understood and within that person's frame of reference. It's about helping that person process the information in a way that makes sense and clearly articulates the relevance for that person.

Consider Anne, a CFO for a small electronics manufacturer. She routinely presented the company's financial data to the management team, to the board of directors, and to the company's employees. In each case, she delivered the same information but she tailored the message for each audience. The internal management team she addressed was composed of three engineers and Anne. The engineers couldn't interpret spreadsheets, so Anne converted the information on the spreadsheets into graphs and tables. For the board, she turned her spreadsheets into balance and income statements, as would appear in an annual report. For the employees, she focused on a few key numbers and showed what the numbers meant to them—Christmas bonuses, layoffs, good shipping and payment flow from customers, etc. She didn't change the underlying facts, but rather found ways to help the different stakeholders make sense of the information. Once they did, she could pursue solving an issue or getting a decision made.

SHAPING THE MESSAGE

So, where do you begin? First, consider your audience, and then connect with the various stakeholders to understand their needs and possible interests. Next, you need to use what you have learned about the primary interests of your stakeholders to help match your message to what concerns them, excites them, scares them, or may enable or inhibit them from moving forward and supporting your challenge or project. Based on their concerns and interests, evaluate where and how you need to focus, such as on competitive data, financial outcomes, or staffing effects. If you have difficulty tailoring your message for particular stakeholders, you may not have learned enough about that group. Take the time to learn more about these stakeholders instead of moving forward based on your own assumptions.

Shifting the focus of the story to what is most important for individual stakeholders will help engage them in your challenge. Remember, being involved doesn't guarantee that they will immediately agree with your approach and offer their full support going forward. Indeed, that should not be your goal or expectation. Rather, your goal in engaging them should be their willingness to participate in a

dialogue with you. You need to recognize the importance of their expertise and knowledge in crafting a shared, sustainable solution.

Each stakeholder group or individual represents a unique piece
of the puzzle that you are trying to assemble into a coherent picture.
As you talk with your stakeholders, your story should evolve and develop with their input, increasing the likelihood of a better solution.
You want them to be able and willing to carry the message forward
to specific audiences.

The development of the story is iterative—by repeating it, adjusting the message, and incorporating stakeholders' input, you'll be
able to craft a message that appeals at some level to all of your stakeholders. As you speak with each stakeholder, incorporate what you
learn into your message. Think about your favorite story to tell at parties. It has evolved as you have learned to tell it better, knowing what
to emphasize, what to describe in more detail, and what to leave out
entirely. By telling it again and again, you have learned how to make
it entertaining, informative, and engaging.

In addition to tailoring the focus of your message to address the
interests of the stakeholder groups, think about the logistics of how
you deliver your story, that is, the location and the amount of time
that you will have, as well as the desired outcome of each interaction.
Just as you do in building relationships, think about how you can best
use every opportunity to strengthen the stakeholder's connection to
the work that has to be done.

You likely have a formal presentation ready for scheduled events
where you have the floor and an hour to tell the full story. In these
situations, the audience knows what you will be talking about and is
ready, even if they disagree, to listen to your presentation. They generally know why they are there and what to expect. Although re-
hearsed presentations like this may offer the best opportunity to tell
the "full story," chances are you will have only brief conversations
with some key individuals whose support is critical. These may be
unexpected encounters or scheduled meetings where you find you
only have a few minutes to share your message and influence their
perspective. In meetings, you may have 20 minutes to present your
message according to an agenda. However, meetings often deviate
from their agendas. You need to be prepared to communicate your
message in a concise way because you may be reduced to the final

few minutes of an executive committee meeting or 2 minutes with an individual before he or she has to rush off to another appointment. Be ready to quickly adjust the story to fit the moment.

THE ELEVATOR VERSION

In some cases, the message needs to be concise because there's a limited amount of time to get the key points across and engage someone in your challenge. Here, the story should consist of pertinent information, with the focus of the story complementing the real interest of the stakeholder. Like any good story, there should be a hook—some reason the person will be intrigued, interested, concerned—a way to engage the person emotionally to care about the outcome. Elevator speeches, which are those one to two minutes of quick selling that you should be able to deliver during an elevator ride, are often associated with people trying to sell something, such as a consulting service or themselves if they are looking for a job. When engaging stakeholders, you also need to be ready with the "elevator" version of your story.

The Babcock Elevator Competition, an annual event hosted by Wake Forest University in Winston-Salem, North Carolina, takes this challenge of crafting a concise message to the "reality" level. Thirty plus teams of MBA students from Wake Forest, Duke, Carnegie Mellon, and other universities gather at a downtown office building. Each team of two has two minutes, or 28 floors, which is the length of time it takes to ride the elevator to the top of the building, to intrigue a real venture capitalist (five of whom spend the day riding up and down the elevator listening to student pitches). No props are allowed, no handouts—the student's business plan must have the critical elements that would appeal to a venture capitalist. At the 28th floor, or when the stopwatch clocks two minutes, time is up. The only thing they can leave behind is a business card.

The reward for this challenge? Six teams are selected to receive an additional 20 minutes to present their business plans to the group of venture capitalists. The ultimate winner gets an introduction to a venture capitalist specializing in the winning team's area of business. In the five years that the program has been active, at least four of the businesses promoted were actually launched. (Hilgers, 2004)

What makes a good elevator pitch and takes an MBA team to the final round? *The clear presentation of a particular problem and a corresponding solution to that problem.* The venture capitalists involved in the Babcock Elevator Competition responded to business plans that sparked their interest and they were drawn to the plans that presented clear pictures of the problem and an innovative solution.

This "two-minute elevator talk" is a good way to think about scaling your message to your stakeholders. If your message is limited to two minutes, then you must really understand the stakeholders and focus on their key concerns. Using the stakeholder analysis, you should be able to identify what will spark each person's interest.

Haitian Healthcare Songs: Story of Matthew Baugh

Sometimes understanding your stakeholders means taking into account their personal situations. Matthew Baugh is a Duke University graduate and Rhodes Scholar. During a trip to Haiti, he brainstormed with medical staff about ways to deliver public health messages to a populace that was largely illiterate. Using his musical background, he collaborated with the staff to craft the health messages as song lyrics in the native language set to music, and broadcast them over the local radio station. They thought that rhyme and music would be the best way for this group to remember the messages they wanted to teach them.

Baugh and his team picked the most common health needs and used a mix of musical styles to create songs about hypertension, songs about supplies to have on hand for labor and delivery (as the majority of babies were still born at home), songs about how often to come in to the clinics for de-worming medications, and even songs about preventing common ailments such as diarrhea. Baugh said he knew that his team had been successful when he heard village children singing one of the health songs they had heard on the radio. (Simon, NPR, 2000)

What results are you hoping to get out of an "elevator speech"? In the case of the MBA students' presentations, their goal was to generate enough interest to be allowed to present a second time and give more details of their story. Consider one sales presentation team who was approaching an important first meeting with a key account that they had been courting for some time. They had a similar goal to that of the students. Before entering the initial meeting, one of the junior presenters asked the head of business development: "What do we want the outcome of this meeting to be?" His answer: "A second meeting."

ADAPTING TO STAKEHOLDERS' PERSONAL STYLES

At some point in your career you may have encountered a type of personal assessment tool designed to gain insight to your own values, preferences, and behaviors. All of these contribute to your leadership style and preferred methods for getting work done. The personal preferences, values, and behavior tendencies of your stakeholders will affect their decision-making styles as well. As you are considering how you will adapt your message for different stakeholders, think also about how your stakeholder will "experience" that message, what their personal styles may be. There are several different types of stakeholders to consider.

- *Enthusiast.* Open to new ideas and trying new approaches. Enthusiastic, optimistic, a "big picture" visionary or entrepreneur. Likely to look for and take advantage of new opportunities that are tightly connected to the strategy.
- *Evaluator.* Cautious, but willing to take calculated risks if the facts support it. Will want to see the supporting data and give careful analysis.
- *Skeptic.* Risk averse and not willing to rock the boat. Follows the "if it ain't broke, don't fix it" approach. Doesn't consider all new ideas as "advances."
- *Angler.* Less concerned about the project itself and more concerned about the political implications and personal benefits

of involvement. Interested in what he or she can gain by engaging in the challenge. Looks for all the angles.

Consider your stakeholder map and analysis. In addition to taking into account their desired and current support levels and issues, which style of thinking is most applicable to each of your stakeholders? How will you tailor your approach and message to bring them into alignment with your strategy?

To draw in those people who are more open to new ideas, you will need to keep the message simple and direct. Focus on the future—these are your visionaries, who can see the potential and work to make it happen. Explain how the project links to their overall vision and strategy. Make the connections simple to understand and talk about "enhancing the upside."

In our Olympic Games example from Chapter 4, our bid driver, Billy Payne, needed to draw in one of the city's most dynamic leaders—the Mayor. In analyzing his stakeholder map, Payne knew that the Mayor's endorsement and alignment with the project would be critical to getting others to join in with their support, including other civic leaders; the 46,000 volunteers that would be needed to make the event happen; the city transportation, water and sewer, and power departments; and others. Without developing a message tailored to appeal to this charismatic leader—a message that was simple, forward-thinking, and pushing toward the overall strategy of landing the city on the international map—Payne could easily have offended or "snubbed" this stakeholder and, ultimately, doomed his project.

With the more skeptical and risk-averse stakeholders, be conscious of their tendency to rely on what's been tested and proven. To create a message for this group, you need to know how your project aligns with things done in the past. Making those "historical precedent" connections will be essential for you to get your message across. Once the skeptic understands how the project came about, and what has been accomplished to this point, you're more likely to gain alignment. Make the message credible; the skeptic will be looking for the risks involved. Along that line, you also need to acknowledge and address the downside risks and explain how you will work to reduce those risks.

Consider the resistance Payne received from a major group of skeptics, the editorial board of the local daily newspaper. These individuals were more inclined to shoot his dream down by selling newspapers filled with stories of the downside to hosting such an event, the problems that were likely to occur, how bad the event could make the city look when it failed (note the "when," not "if," attitude), and historic stories of failures in other cities. This group could be considered Payne's harshest critic; however, it was vital to the success of the project. By tailoring the message in such a way as to draw allegiance from the group, he could impact how this very vocal group carried the message forward.

So what did Payne do? He focused on the positives: how the city had accomplished major activities in the past through drawing residents, corporations, elected officials, and others together to achieve a common goal. He referenced specifics, be it the success of attracting a major national sports team to the area or citizens coming together to create a huge project like a convention center. He talked about reducing the risks by explaining what the risks were and how they would be addressed. He acknowledged the challenges, and then presented the solutions.

You might consider those who want supporting data as the real challenge. Their reliance on facts and proven success could be a stumbling block if your solution is unconventional, but if you shape the message to show how it could work, they could become your best supporters.

Billy Payne focused on swaying some of the most reluctant stakeholders he could imagine—the city's transportation department. With limited funding, ongoing challenges, and demands from the public to improve public transportation, roads, and bridges, and a critical public, the transportation department was resistant to the project. After all, such an event would bring thousands of athletes and coaches and 45,000 volunteers to the area, it would require moving 500,000 to 600,000 people a day to venues around the city, and all of this would happen during a relentless 18-day period while businesses continue to operate.

Payne, knowing what type of group he would be addressing, acknowledged the challenge, and pointed out the facts as they were realized by other U.S. cities involved in the Olympics in the past. Armed with the statistics and other data, he was able to communicate with the group and get their agreement and support of the challenge.

BUILDING A PERSONALIZED MESSAGE

By tailoring your message and approach to fit your stakeholders' personal styles, you have a greater chance of bringing each of them on board to work with you toward the best solution to your challenge.

CHECKLIST

❏ Have you developed tailored versions of your story to match stakeholder interests?

❏ Have you prepared an "elevator" version?

❏ Have you considered your stakeholders' personal styles?

❏ Are you prepared to adapt your story to accommodate those who
  - are eager to take on new strategic challenges?
  - are less reluctant to change what is comfortable?
  - want supporting data before acting?
  - are concerned about the political implications of participating?

CHAPTER SEVEN

CREATING A SHARED STORY

IN THIS CHAPTER

The Evolving Story ■ Creating an Open Invitation ■ Balancing Advocacy and Inquiry ■ Putting the Pieces Together ■ Conflicts and Challenges Are Inevitable ■ Building a Shared Story

When people truly share a vision, they are connected, bound together by a common aspiration. . . . In fact, we have come to believe that one of the reasons people seek to build shared visions is their desire to be connected in an important undertaking. (Senge, 1994)

"Every picture tells a story," to quote Rod Stewart . . . and every story should help stakeholders envision a picture of future success. Leaders need to develop clear, easily communicated stories to frame the challenges they are facing and draw in stakeholders to the "action." But how do you do this?

THE EVOLVING STORY

By now, you know the impact that storytelling can have in getting others engaged in your challenge—how a simple story can convey your message. Think of the first version of the story that you have created as a rough draft. It's not complete and you still have a lot of work to do. The best stories will be ones that evolve from a collaborative process, incorporating the bits and pieces of your stakeholders' knowledge, experiences, and creativity, and lead to the development of a shared story. Much like a live performance, each time you tell the story will be unique, drawing on the perspective and mood of the "audience." Based on feedback from each delivery, you'll incorporate new ideas that seem to work well and replace other content that does not seem to fit.

The creation of this shared story brings stakeholders into the team, and allows them to carry your vision to others as they retell it. Hopefully, it will be a rallying vision that they can easily make their own and deliver to other internal and external stakeholders.

Keep Your Stories Fresh

Even though stories change and adapt as we tell them multiple times, you may feel as if the story is getting "old." But remember, your stakeholders are hearing the story for the first time. When he retired after 30 years as an artist and manager with Hallmark Cards, the late Gordon MacKenzie had been given the title "Creative Paradox" and had a reputation within the company as a wonderful storyteller.

In retirement, he turned this into a new job as a full-time presenter and storyteller, but with a unique approach. He would begin his delivery standing in front of a clothesline that held several drawings. Each drawing represented a different story and the audience could pick which drawing he took down and, thus, which story he told. No matter how many times he did this, the stories seemed fresh, perhaps because the audience was actively engaged in the process and hearing them for the first time. Eventually, he would pretend to hear the audience choose the last drawing that read simply "Let's Do Something Else," and the presentation would come to a close. (Ganzel, 1999)

CREATING AN OPEN INVITATION

Your challenge in creating a compelling invitation is twofold. First, you must make sure that there is an open place at the table for everyone to feel a part of the process. Second, you should provide an opportunity for the team to exchange ideas. Are there enough opportunities for everyone to participate and interact? The invitations should be extended to stakeholders not just to allow them to listen to you, but to give them the opportunity to participate in a dialogue—for you to tell your story and for them to react and respond. Make sure you book enough time for both the delivery of the message and for your audience to provide input. Often, people underestimate the time it takes to tell their story.

In telling your story, remember that the "hard sell" is out. If you take that route, your audience is likely to close their minds to whatever you're saying. With the hard sell, you are selling a version of your story as a "done deal," without taking into consideration any stakeholder contributions. Sure, if you've worked through the stakeholder map, you now know your stakeholders. But you are just beginning to find out about their experiences, thoughts, and ideas regarding the situation at hand. You must be open to learning more about your stakeholders, acknowledge them, and incorporate their input to create the shared story.

Create an invitation that encourages them to envision and consider the realm of possibilities, rather than only listening to a presentation of your view.

You've worked through your own responses to the guiding questions that we set forth in Chapter 5, but only when you elicit and incorporate your stakeholders' points of view as well will you really begin to build a shared story. How do *they* view the current situation, opportunities, or priorities? What risks are *they* most concerned about? What benefits do *they* envision? What does all of this mean for *them*?

Consider what an NCAA Championship basketball coach did with her team. She told them at the beginning of the year that if they kept focused, they would win the national championship. She stressed their skills, the way the schedule had been set up, and how nice it would be for the senior star to finish "March Madness" in her

.

hometown where the Final Four was going to be held. The coach set up the possible ending to the season, and then allowed the team captains and the rest of the team to fill in how they would win the national title game. The team found a rallying cry and song that helped unify and motivate them. Each player was able to add her own contribution to the story based on her position and role on the team: helping others improve their skills, giving 100% hustle in practice, or playing each game of the year as a warm-up for the finals. The result of their combined involvement: The team won the National Championship, with a 32-1 record for the season.

Remember, this is a collaborative process. First, use your relationships: What have you learned so far from your stakeholders? What's important to each of them? How does that interest correspond with the story you are crafting? How can you approach individual stakeholders and get them to add to the story?

Next, using what you know about your stakeholders, "create the invitation" for input. Present stakeholders with your challenge and begin the dialogue. Here's where you begin creating the shared story. By communicating issues of shared interest, you can open the door to gaining input from stakeholders.

BALANCING ADVOCACY AND INQUIRY

As you begin communicating with stakeholders, you'll need to balance advocating your own interests and point of view with inquiring and learning about theirs. Avoid relying too heavily on one approach. When you *only inquire,* you prevent others from learning about your views, you don't build rapport, and people might begin to feel interrogated. On the other hand, when you *only advocate,* you won't learn about potential flaws in your own thinking, about the person's reasoning or data, and others might feel berated or irrelevant (as in, "Why are you even asking me if you already have the answer?").

Use what you already know about your stakeholders to help you determine what the right balance will be for each group. Figure 7.1 reviews the five levels of stakeholder support, which were introduced in Chapter 4, and how to approach each type.

FIGURE 7.1 Applying Advocacy and Inquiry Techniques

Stakeholder	Advocacy Approach	Inquiry Approach
Active Supporter (2)	Reinforce the benefits of achieving your vision and enlist these people to elaborate on the ideas.	Use inquiry to learn even more about their views and potential ways in which they can help further.
Passive Supporter (1)	Advocate your position if you need a higher level of support from these individuals.	Inquire to learn if there are reasons preventing their full support.
Neutral Supporter (0)	Relate the challenge and your story in a neutral way.	After sharing your story, ask for feedback or concerns.
Passive Resistor (–1)	Decide if you or some-one else should approach each person. Begin with inquiry before respond-ing with advocacy.	Validate that they are resisting. Inquire to learn more about why.
Active Resistor (–2)	Avoid advocating. Decide who should approach each person.	Validate that you understand the real reasons behind their resistance. Inquire to try and learn more.

Advocating involves taking others through your thought process and explaining how you came to the opinion that you now hold. An appropriate approach to advocating your opinion would be as follows:

- Start the discussion by providing your audience with your assumptions about a situation and any data that back up your assumption. *"Here's what I think, and here's how I got there. . . ."*

- Explain your assumptions to clarify them for your stakeholder. *"I assume that. . . ."*
- Be very clear about how you reached a certain conclusion. *"I came to this conclusion because. . . ."*
- Explain the context of your story, and who will be affected, how, and why. *"To get a clear picture of what I'm talking about, put yourself in the customer's shoes. . . ."*
- Share examples of what you propose, even if solutions are hypothetical. This helps present the invitation to the dialogue. *"Here's what I was thinking. . . ."*

Inquiring involves encouraging others to explain their thought processes and the basis for their opinions. Begin your inquiry using the following techniques:

- Find out what data your stakeholder is interpreting to understand the situation, but do this in a gentle, nonaggressive way. *"I really want to understand how you came to that conclusion. What kind of information do you have (that supports this conclusion)?"*
- Ask questions in a way that doesn't promote defensiveness. *"Can you help me understand your thinking here?"* (NOT: *What's your proof?*)
- Draw out the reasoning for the position and find out as much as you can about why the person is saying what he or she is saying. *"Help me understand the significance of that. How does this relate to your other concerns?"*
- Explain your reasons for inquiry and how your questions relate to your own concerns, hopes, and needs. *"I'm asking you about your assumptions here because. . . ."*

You've made your thinking process known; now it's time for you to find out more about your stakeholders' thinking processes. Be careful to practice *active listening* as they respond to your inquiries. Active listening requires a different set of skills. You need to consciously make the effort to engage with others and to express respect, concern, concentration, and a desire to understand throughout the course of the conversation.

"To listen well is as powerful a means of influence as to talk well,
and is as essential to all true conversation."
Chinese proverb

Use *active listening* as your main tool to create the shared story. Use the following techniques to ensure that you are actively listening:

- *Seek* the other person's views. Find out what kind of information he or she has. Tread lightly—you should show you are genuinely interested in the other person's ideas and experiences. Make sure you speak in a nonaggressive way because you are aiming to come to a collaborative solution.

The Don'ts:
- Don't be thinking about what you're going to say next—you're supposed to be listening.
- Don't think of other unrelated things—no staring out the window or replaying last night's game. It will be obvious to the person talking (glazed eyes and a slack jaw are giveaways!).
- Don't project your own feelings and ideas on the other person—you're seeking input, not trying to win points.

The Do's
- *Paraphrase* what the person has said to show you understand her views. Ask if there is more information (e.g., "Can you say more about that?"). Draw out the reasoning behind the other person's positions. Make sure you have heard everything that person wants to say about the situation.
- *Validate* the other person's reactions to show you recognize the importance of his views. Acknowledge strong emotion. This doesn't mean you agree with the point or share the emotion, but rather that you understand this person's feeling and it is legitimate for him or her to have it.
- *Empathize* with the other person to show you are concerned with his of her position.

Remember that at this stage, you are listening and responding to your stakeholders. This is *not* the time to declare a solution at the end of each exchange. Stakeholder comments, ideas, or experiences may alter your original point of view about a problem. You are still shaping the story—and you still have other stakeholders to approach. Proposing solutions or particular points of view as "final" is premature at this point and could damage credibility down the road.

The Listener's Role

Two experiments were conducted to test the collaborative theory of narrative storytelling—what listeners do and their effect on the narrator. The test group consisted of 81 women and 45 men. They were divided into 63 unacquainted pairs, with one person acting as narrator and the other as listener. The narrator told the listener a personal "close call" story, and the listeners were instructed to make one of two different kinds of responses: generic responses, including nodding and murmuring sounds such as "mhm," or specific responses, such as wincing or exclaiming, directly tied to what the narrator was saying at the time.

When listeners were less responsive during the experiment, the narrators told their stories significantly less well, particularly at the dramatic end of the close-call story. The researchers concluded that listeners acted as "co-narrators," both through their own specific responses, which helped illustrate the story, and in their effect upon the narrator's performance. The results demonstrated the importance of moment-by-moment collaboration in face-to-face dialogue. (Bavelas, 2000)

PUTTING THE PIECES TOGETHER

Next, present the pros and cons of different ideas to your stakeholders. In doing this, you need to acknowledge their input on the solution. You've digested their insights; you've thought about the risks and alternatives. By verbalizing your process, you strengthen the relationship with your stakeholders, increasing the likelihood of a shared solution.

Make sure your stakeholders know their input has mattered. You're not presenting them with the solution to a problem, but rather, you're asking for their input, incorporating their ideas and experiences, and coming up with a collaborative solution. You're building on existing relationships, with new information gathered through the active listening process, to create this shared story.

Think about how the collaborative story can bridge gaps. It goes back to the idea of relationship-building: Once a common ground is found (the collaborative story), an acceptance and positive energy begins to flow among stakeholders. By acknowledging and incorporating their input, you've given stakeholders their part in the solution. This leads to greater buy-in and credibility.

CONFLICTS AND CHALLENGES ARE INEVITABLE

In the Clark Fork River project, a shared story led to a successful project. However, sharing doesn't always go well. As we work with others, there is the potential for conflict. Your story can develop plot twists, both from events and from the environment.

Let's look at global strategy teams in the pharmaceutical industry. These teams are set up within a company to integrate activities and allocate resources across all functions in the organization—from research to development to regulatory to manufacturing to marketing to sales—and across all geographies involved in a given therapeutic area. These cross-functional teams determine the entire business' success; how well a molecule is managed from discovery to pharmacy ties directly to how much profit a drug will provide before its patent expires. Delayed FDA (and equivalents) approval, slow sales, supply delays, and competitor generics can cost the company billions of dollars if the drug is a big seller.

All large, global, multitherapeutic area pharmaceutical companies have some form of this critical cross-functional team. It is also true that across all of them, these teams are struggling to work effectively. In a sense, the deck is stacked against them. Partly due to long product development cycles and partly due to highly technical jobs, much of the key work of pharmaceutical companies occurs within functional groups. People often stay within a functional group throughout their entire career, developing deep professional identities and deep expertise with their own language and culture.

The Clark Fork River Project

Avista Corporation used a collaborative relicensing process that has revolutionized the way hydroelectric power companies work with their stakeholders. The Clark Fork River, in Missoula, Montana, was up for relicensing from the Federal Energy Regulatory Commission (FERC). The process can oftentimes be contentious because it involves a number of disparate stakeholders, including federal government officials, state agencies, Native American Tribes, conservation groups, and the like. In mid-1996, Avista officials decided to try something new and take a collaborative approach that would develop protection, mitigation, and enhancement measures to form a comprehensive settlement agreement amongst all stakeholders.

Thus was born the Clark Fork Relicensing Team (CFRT). It was made up of more than 40 organizations, including federal and state agencies from Idaho and Montana, 5 Native American Tribes, nongovernment organizations, conservation groups, property owners, and Avista Corp. The CRFT stakeholders subdivided into five areas:

1. Fisheries technical work group

2. Water resources technical work group

3. Wildlife, wetlands, and botanical technical work group

4. Land use, recreation, and aesthetics technical work group

5. Cultural resources management group

Tim Swant, who represented Avista during the process and was responsible for implementing the terms of the new FERC license, noted that once they were actually in the implementation phase, they were even more appreciative of the collaborative process. Chip Corsi of Idaho Fish and Game agreed that trust developed early on and continued throughout the project.

When asked about any downsides to the collaborative process, Swant did admit to worrying about how changes in personnel among the stakeholders would affect the collaborative process. There was concern that much of the historical knowledge and experience of stakeholders who had worked through two-plus years of consultation would be lost.

But the problem became a nonissue, because the management committee, made up of 27 stakeholders, collectively took up the responsibility of mentoring stakeholders by training, educating, nurturing, and orienting new members. This management committee actively participated in keeping the group working toward relicensing.

Corsi noted that the people Avista put in charge of making the relicensing process work were people that inspired trust and confidence—they allowed the participants to collectively make decisions that they would then follow through to completion. (Ayer, 2001)

In this example, an effort was made to incorporate all stakeholders in the process. Their perspectives were considered and they were brought into the process from the beginning. This openness and respect for the players energized them. What could have been a monumental challenge was solved efficiently as a result of their collaborative efforts. Each stakeholder had a place at the table, was heard and respected, and became part of the solution. By knowing which stakeholders made up their "big picture," the management committee was able to address concerns and issues of both internal and external stakeholders.

Also, because the work is often done within functions, budgeting and goal setting processes also take place in the functions. So, knowledge, language, identity, and incentives all serve to support working within function, not within the cross-functional team. Physical distance and time availability don't help much either. Often team members are globally dispersed—some working while others are asleep. Because they are among the most effective managers within their functions, they also are extremely busy in their normal roles. Together, these factors lead to three types of conflict within these global strategy teams: strategy, performance, and identity.

1. *Problems of strategy.* In a cross-functional team, members come in with different training, priorities, and interpretations. When an opportunity presents itself, team members may interpret it very differently; one may see the next great advance while another views it as a likely dead end that should no longer be funded. Members may interpret events and set priorities using different and potentially conflicting perspectives.

2. *Problems of performance.* Recall that the purpose of global strategy teams is to make key strategic decisions regarding priorities, coordinate tasks, and allocate resources. Once an agreement is reached, the separate functions execute their parts. Here the trouble begins, as inevitably one of the functions is required to change a priority, give something up, or add work to an already busy schedule. For agreements to hold, each member of the team needs to be able to deliver an assigned function. However, more often than not, these team members do not run the function; they have no formal authority to insist on a priority change or that resources be reallocated. They set expectations across the organization that they alone can't ensure come off well. Instead they need to work with, cajole, plead, and in other ways influence their functional colleagues to get things to happen. If even one team member fails to persuade his or her function, then the whole agreement or project is at risk. With busy schedules and demanding roles, members don't always see a clear way to meet the expectations. As a result, tasks critical to the team's work sometimes do not get done.

3. *Problems of identity.* People have a strong need for affiliation and belonging. We need to identify ourselves with a group. With the global strategy teams, the members can be conflicted about their identities. Although they are typically proud of being asked to be on such a critical team, they also primarily identify with their functional role. They are scientists or marketers first, and members of a team second (or third). The organization doesn't help; their functions may resist the cross-functional teams' plans and the existing budgeting and incentive processes reward functional work, not cross-

functional work. It becomes personally risky to invest in being part of the global strategy team.

These three problems are not unique to pharmaceutical planning teams. Rather, many groups face the same issues. As a manager, you may confront such conflicts as you try to build a shared story. Some people won't see how they can perform in the framework you lay out. Some will disagree with your view of the opportunities or how to capitalize on them. Others may see a personal risk if asked to act outside their area of expertise or connections.

When conflicts do occur, situations and conversations become more challenging. We noted the research of John Gottman and his colleagues at University of Washington in Chapter 3. They can predict (with 91 percent accuracy) the probability of divorce by observing how couples talk about a sensitive or emotionally charged topic. This may be the most powerful result in all of the social sciences: Critical conversations serve as the basis for defining a relationship and demonstrate how we work with each other in other aspects of the relationship.

As you are developing a shared story, you may face some challenging conversations with stakeholders. You may see the opportunity differently, or you may not have the goodwill you thought you did. The other may misinterpret your request, or feel uncomfortable with being asked. We've already mentioned balancing advocacy and inquiry as one consideration for having a constructive dialogue. That considers what is said, but not how it's interpreted. A conversation can stall at exactly the wrong moment if emotions or goodwill get exhausted. As a simple rule of thumb, in a conversation:

The level of negative emotion aroused + The level of
effort required to reach agreement should be < The
level of goodwill in the relationship

If it gets too hard or too negative, it's time to try a different approach.

To build a shared story, you need to have a relationship and some common concerns. Next, ensure that you have the goodwill to engage each other effectively. Then, when conversations become challenging, follow these guidelines (from Gottman, et al) to help keep them on the right track and maintain the relationship.

- *Attractive invitation.* Create a genuine and attractive invitation to the discussion and gauge the depth of effort and introspection in which your partners are willing to engage. A weak invitation brings unwilling parties to the table and risks creating even further problems if the parties leave the discussion at just the wrong point, when problems seem the worst. Difficult discussions taken too deep or grappled with too quickly can also undo a relationship. As a simple example, you don't discuss _____ on a first date.

- *Balanced conversation.* If you watch casual conversations, there is a clear balance in who speaks for how long, and a seamless shift from one topic to the next. No one is "in charge" of the conversation and thus no one dominates. Charged conversations easily lose one of these features. Gottman's research shows that couples who talk past each other (an unsynchronized chat), have emotions escalate, or have one party dominating are more likely to divorce. So too in work discussions.

- *Seek explanations.* Ask others to explain their opinions and give reasons for your own. It is amazing how often people assert their position and simply expect others to understand. Seek to learn more about their frame of reference. Ask yourself, why is this conversation also difficult for them?

- *Soften the message.* Tough stuff hurts; be sure to soften the message in genuine ways. This is not the old "start with the good stuff before slamming someone." Be sensitive to the effect your words have on another person and use language that allows that person to actually hear the difficult messages.

- *De-escalate situations.* When things begin to get out of hand, have the skill to pause, diffuse the situation, and take the conversation back to a manageable level. Remember, a discussion should only exist at the level of goodwill created between the parties. Take a break, change the topic or the scope of the discussion, or use humor.

- *Reinstate goodwill.* When it is over, do something to ensure that the goodwill you had is not damaged. Go have a beer together, go to a sporting or cultural event, take a walk, or shake hands. Do something to rebuild any lost goodwill and signal that you are both okay.

BUILDING A SHARED STORY

Take what you learn from each interaction and conversation with stakeholders and incorporate their experiences and expertise into a collective solution. At this point, focus on energizing your stakeholders around the challenge, even if this means making it overtly clear how they impacted the solution.

CHECKLIST

☐ Create a compelling invitation for stakeholders to participate with an extended "guest list."

☐ Balance advocating your point of view with learning about others' points of view.

☐ Make sure you are *really* listening.

☐ Incorporate others' ideas into the story.

☐ If conflicts and challenging conversations do occur, see explanations and take steps to de-escalate the situation.

☐ Take care to rebuild any goodwill that was lost.

CHAPTER EIGHT

BUILDING CREDIBILITY AND DEEPENING YOUR NETWORK

IN THIS CHAPTER

The Trust Equation ■ Relationships Begin with
Credibility ■ A Leader's Credibility ■ Taking It to the Next
Level ■ Managing the Unexpected ■ Staying Connected

Two themes have been prevalent throughout this book: the need
to simultaneously focus energy on building and sustaining your network of relationships and on creating the best solutions and results
for the organization. This means recognizing the interdependencies
and connections between the people involved and the work you need
to accomplish.

We've talked about taking those first steps in building relationships by initiating and taking advantage of opportunities to connect
and interact. We've noted the importance of having productive conversations that balance advocating your own point of view with actively and genuinely inquiring and listening to others' interests and
opinions. We've also covered the impact of creating a shared story of
what success looks like in building collaborative solutions. All of
these play a part in building and strengthening relationships with
stakeholders across your network.

Think back to the example in Chapter 3 where we mapped the
initial relationships with the various stakeholders associated with a

project. Those relationships likely existed on multiple levels—missing, weak, developing, strong—and had different characteristics in terms of duration, familiarity, purpose, and perceived outcome, just as your own relationships do. If a stakeholder relationship has become a strong one, chances are you not only have proven credible and reliable, but also have shared some of your personal stories in connection to the issues being discussed. You likely have demonstrated that you are concerned about their interests as well as your own.

THE TRUST EQUATION

In their work on developing client relationships, the authors of *The Trusted Advisor* outline the phases of relationship development that those in a service role and their clients evolve through before reaching the highest level—the trust relationship. They describe relationships that begin as service-based where the focus is on the provider (you) supplying answers, expertise, and information to the customer (your stakeholder) that are on time and accurate. In other words, can they trust what you say? Those relationships then can strengthen to higher levels that focus first on building solutions and then move on to generating new ideas and insights for the stakeholder's organization. The highest trust-based relationship will reach a level that focuses on the stakeholder as an individual and creates a "safe" environment for discussing the hard issues. (Maister, Green, and Galford, 2000)

Although you are not likely to nor do you need to develop each stakeholder relationship to that level of trust, there are some key factors that are applicable to all relationships. Maister, Green, and Galford have developed the Trust Equation to think about how these key factors will impact any given relationship:

$$\text{Trust} = \frac{\text{Credibility} + \text{Reliability} + \text{Intimacy}}{\text{Self-orientation}}$$

RELATIONSHIPS BEGIN WITH CREDIBILITY

Relationships develop in different ways and not all need be the same, but they all should begin with *credibility*. If you can't pass this first test with stakeholders, it is unlikely that you will be allowed to develop the relationship any further. Relationships develop over time and evolve through a combination of perceived attributes, such as your honesty, credentials, competence, experience, reliability, and motives. Think about why you watch a particular newscaster, read a particular newspaper, use a certain stockbroker, or seek out a particular colleague for an opinion. Odds are these sources have provided reliable, consistent information over a period of time, reinforcing your belief in them as trusted advisors. If there have been times when they have had to correct previous statements, you have appreciated the way that they communicated this to you. They have been able to deal with and recover from the occasional misstep because their actions during both good times and bad have worked to build their credibility with you.

Each opportunity you have to interact with stakeholders is also an opportunity to strengthen their perceptions of your credibility. With some stakeholders, you will have many chances at building and strengthening your relationship and credibility. With others, you may only have a single opportunity. Your challenge is to make the most of each interaction, remembering that they hopefully are part of an additive, long-term relationship.

As you approach each challenge or project, think beyond the work at hand and be cognizant of the ways in which your interactions will build or damage your credibility. Without credibility, you lose your ability to be successful in the role of translator and, ultimately, your ability to influence and collaborate for results.

A LEADER'S CREDIBILITY

How you build credibility parallels building relationships. Both are processes involving interactions with your stakeholders. Both rely on previous information to make new gains. Both are essential to your success in influencing and collaborating for results. Because people form opinions based on their experiences with you and use these opinions in future decision making and in influencing others' opinions, you must constantly work on building and maintaining credibility.

The old saying "you have to have credit to get credit" is often true. On their own, today's 20-something generation is finding that they are often turned down by banks for small loans or credit cards, and often have to rely on their parents to vouch for their credibility in paying back their debts. However, some people can't even borrow someone else's credit to get credit.

Professor Muhammad Yanus sought to turn these standard banking rules around in Bangladesh in 1976 when the country was suffering from severe famine. Professor Yanus appealed to local banks to help poor villagers, but they declined to loan even very small amounts of money—as little as one dollar per person—to people who were illiterate and had no real collateral. Against everyone's warnings, he took out loans himself and loaned his own money to poor village women so that they could invest in the livestock and materials they needed to survive and make money of their own. These loans were repaid, and he made more loans, expanding to other villages and districts.

In 1983, the Grameen Bank was formally created. Instead of requiring collateral, the bank gives loans to the poor on a group liability basis. To qualify, in addition to being poor, the prospective borrower must find five friends to borrow with. Initial loans are typically $10 to $20 and are made to one or two members of the group. The bank requires both small weekly installments and a mandatory savings plan, which is as little as a few pennies per week. As the loans are repaid and the group builds credibility, the loan amounts may be increased and loans are then extended to the other members of the group.

The bank's theory is that those who are too poor to get regular bank loans *are* good credit bets, and they appear to have been proven right as the loan collection rate is nearly 98 percent. As the borrowers are able to provide more income through their loans, the loans are repaid, the group gains credibility, and, in turn, is given more credit—creating a positive cycle. Once they say they will repay a loan and actually do it, their credibility has grown. As a result of the Bank, women have raised their status, lessened their dependency on their husbands, and improved the lives of their families.

How do you create actions and associations that exhibit your credibility? What do these terms really mean? How do people evaluate them? How can you as a leader improve the key characteristics that will enhance your credibility?

In describing the complex process of developing trust, *The Trusted Advisor* describes the fine distinction between the "rational" and "emotional" aspects of credibility. The rational side evaluates how accurate or believable you are. Stakeholders can double-check the accuracy of your facts and data or verify your claims with others' direct experiences fairly quickly and without a lot of effort. For example, if you relate a story of a successful project interaction with another stakeholder, it is relatively easy to verify the facts by talking with that person. If your facts and information are verified as accurate, then your other stakeholders will determine that you are telling the truth.

Your stakeholders may verify that you are accurate with facts and data, but that doesn't automatically mean that they view you as *honest*. The emotional side of credibility is described as one that checks for completeness—not only are you not telling lies, but are you being forthcoming with the entire truth? Your honesty takes longer for stakeholders to assess and thus longer for you to establish. This level of credibility is built mostly through your direct interactions with stakeholders; thus, the need to consider the implications of each opportunity. (Meister, Green, and Galford, 2000)

How do you impact how others view your honesty? The best approach is to anticipate their concerns and needs, and address them directly. Be forthcoming in your conversations with people, acknowledging areas where the challenges will be most difficult, and where there are differences of opinion. When you don't know the answer, admit it.

Honesty is also judged by how well you maintain commitments. When interacting with stakeholders, don't create false expectations or unrealistic commitments. Sometimes people create false impressions because they get careless with their words. They make statements with all good intentions that listeners interpret as promises. When they can't deliver what they seem to have promised, they are then seen as unreliable or dishonest. (Pagano and Pagano, 2004) Avoid making commitments to do things in a certain way or to follow a particular solution, especially during early stakeholder conversations. Making an early commitment you later have to back out of will create an impression that you can't be trusted.

Your honesty also will be judged not just by whether you respond truthfully when asked directly, but by whether you willingly reveal key information. Altering, misrepresenting, and withholding information can hurt your "honesty rating." Keep in mind, however, that honesty does not always mean full disclosure. There may be times when revealing the entire truth might harm others. As a manager, you may have to respond by saying that you know the answer but can't discuss the details of something at that point in time.

In addition to speaking the truth, be prepared to hear the truth. In conversations with stakeholders, encourage and invite ideas for approaching the challenge that are not as "safe." Welcome innovative ideas about how challenges can be met. Seek out new ways of working together, new alliances, new technologies, or new processes, rather than doing things in the way that feels most familiar and comfortable.

Listen and value the input provided by your stakeholders. Perhaps you have been in situations where you thought twice about offering a different opinion, or offered but weren't sure that the input was entirely welcome or fairly considered. Be prepared for difficult conversations, and as the old saying goes, "Don't shoot the messenger." People need to feel that it's safe to tell the truth and that their input is really valued and will be considered. If you invite people to offer their opinions, versions of events, and concerns, then you need to listen. As you have honest conversations with different stakeholders, new information will emerge, along with potentially new approaches and solutions to the challenge.

TAKING IT TO THE NEXT LEVEL

Once you have created a level of credibility with stakeholders, you have an opportunity to take those relationships to the next level—to one that can work on developing shared solutions and generating collaborative ideas. Stakeholder relationships may begin with the credibility of what you say (facts, figures, and stories), but your actions are what will demonstrate your dependability and consistency. In other words, are you reliable? Do you do what you say you are going to do?

Over the past two decades, researchers and coauthors James Kouzes and Barry Posner have conducted interviews with 75,000 managers worldwide—in many different industries, environments, and cultures—asking what personal traits or characteristics they most looked for in a leader. From their initial survey in 1983 to now, the message has essentially been the same. They report that survey responses consistently rank *honesty* as the characteristic most valued. People want leaders who can be trusted, who also are thinking about the direction in which they are leading others, have the right knowledge and skills for the job, and are enthusiastic and clear in communicating their plans for the future. These add up to personal credibility. (Kouzes, 2003)

Just as with credibility, the way that stakeholders view your reliability can have both a "rational" and an "emotional" aspect. On a rational level, stakeholders judge your reliability with data. Do you meet the deadlines you agreed to? Do you deliver the product numbers you promised? If you said that you will include at least two representatives from each department in review meetings, did you actually do that? We also judge reliability by less formal interactions. Do you return calls as promised? Do you complete even minor items on the to-do list that are assigned to you? Do you prepare and share meeting agendas with the full group in advance? Do you call with updates on a regular basis, before being asked?

How do you demonstrate your reliability and competency in managing project work? Leaders who recognize their own limitations, and work to address those gaps in the project are seen as more competent. Assess what competencies are critical to the challenge, such as industry knowledge, technology certifications, regulatory limits, or process training, and work on bringing the right people and right level of expertise to the table to help build a collaborative solution. Make sure that you are incorporating enough diverse opinions and that you haven't omitted any key stakeholders.

What about the *intimacy* factor in the Trust Equation? Just the word "intimacy," when talking about stakeholders, can raise your level of discomfort. What we really mean is that you feel comfortable enough with them to talk about difficult topics, such as budgets, layoffs, mergers, and personnel problems. Think about the topics that you feel somewhat uncomfortable discussing. As your level of discomfort increases, there is probably a smaller circle of people you feel comfortable discussing the topic with. You have reached a certain level of trust with those people. This is not about sharing your private life with stakeholders, but about sharing your personal thoughts and issues regarding the challenge at hand.

The work that has to be done involves people, and therefore human emotions. Some challenges will raise topics that are especially charged and the conversations will need to go beyond the surface of facts, data, and action plans in order to build solutions. A greater level of comfort means that fewer subjects are "barred" from being discussed. Revealing what keeps you awake at night about a project can feel risky, but it lets stakeholders know that it's "safe" to question things and opens the door for them to do the same. Someone has to make the first move, and it's you.

In the Trust Equation, all of the other factors combined are divided by the level of *self-orientation* that you bring to the equation. Even if your Trust Equation's numerator score (credibility + reliability + intimacy) is high with your stakeholders, too much focus on self-interest reduces your total trust score and derails both the relationship and the results. In earlier chapters we talked about the importance of listening to your stakeholders and of learning more about their interests and concerns instead of focusing on your own. The goal is to find and build the best solution for the organization, not for you. Self-orientation is about your level of personal motivation— your own interests and agenda—versus the level of concern and focus you have for the organization and others involved in the challenge. If you approach stakeholder conversations with more desire to look intelligent or to be right or to get their agreement to your predetermined solution than you have desire to really inquire about and listen to their problems and interests, they will know. How? As the authors point out, they'll know by your being unwilling to say you don't know, by trying to give answers too quickly, or by trying to state their problems before they do. What *can* you do? Ask *them* to talk, listen without distractions and resist the temptation to jump to solutions too early.

MANAGING THE UNEXPECTED

Even with the best of intentions, there will be times where your credibility and, potentially, your relationships are threatened. A corporate crisis such as a plant explosion, corporate scandal, or product failure could thrust your project team or company in the spotlight. Or you may have to deliver unwelcome news to your team or stakeholders such as a project has been canceled, funding has been halted, or key staff have been reassigned. Perhaps new developments mean that you are no longer going to be able to deliver what you said you would. Handling difficult situations is still an opportunity to build credibility. Public relations consultants often counsel business owners, executives, and managers on dealing with the media during times of crisis. One of the first rules is to be honest, and that is the best rule of thumb for your network of stakeholders as well.

A classic case of building credibility in difficult times was how Johnson & Johnson handled the Tylenol crisis of 1982. When product tampering caused the deaths of seven people in the Chicago area, middle managers within the company acted quickly in recalling all of its products from store shelves. The company took an estimated $100 million charge against earnings. When a second incident occurred in 1986, they discontinued the sale of capsules and introduced additional product tamper-evident packaging.

Some criticized the action, seeing the recall as an admission of blame. But the public instead saw a company that was prepared to go to great lengths to make sure its product was safe. Although their market share plummeted during the weeks after the recall, it quickly returned to its former level about three months after the crisis. Johnson & Johnson's quick response, their acceptance of responsibility to solve the problem, and their honest approach with the public made the company that much more credible to consumers. They continue to have that credible reputation, as a trusted, caring brand, more than two decades later. If they had rushed to cover their exposure or deny their culpability, the company may have faltered and suffered long-term effects.

Managers throughout the company reacted quickly, aligning their response with their corporate motto of putting the customer first. Instead of a mission statement that hangs on the wall, they have a one-page credo that managers and employees relied on to make countless decisions during the crises. The first lines of their credo read: *We believe our first responsibility is to the doctors, nurses and patients, to mothers and fathers and all others who use our products and services. In meeting their needs everything we do must be of high quality.* The credo guided individual decision makers to independently take the same action—pull the product. It was this action that saved the brand and built trust with the public. (Johnson & Johnson, 2004)

That can't be said for Enron, which, in 2001, became the "poster child" of corporate fraud and deceit. At one time the seventh-largest public company in the United States, Enron collapsed on rumors of billions of dollars of concealed debt and secret business deals. Executives at Enron worked extremely hard—to deny wrongdoing. Their stubborn denials prolonged the media coverage and contributed greatly to the erosion of their credibility and, ultimately, their companies.

STAYING CONNECTED

As you lead from your position in the center—connecting the work and people across your organization or beyond and hopefully achieving the results you envision—celebrate the successes. But don't consider the process complete. Take steps to ensure that the relationship doesn't end when the single project is finished. Things will continue to change and evolve. There will continue to be a steady stream of new strategic directions, new competitors, new stakeholders, and new initiatives that you will be asked to take on. Protect and nurture your credibility and the network of relationships that you have begun to develop so that you are ready when the next challenge arrives.

FIGURE 8.1 Leading from the Center

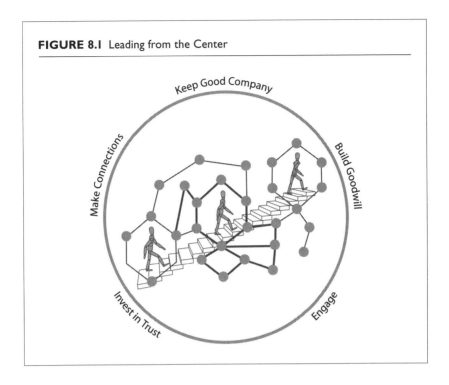

Stay in touch with the people you have made connections with, and keep these relationships fresh. Rather than calling only when *you* want something, call just to check in and see how things are going or to find out what new things they are struggling with. Explore what challenges you may have in common or how other stakeholders in your network might be interested in what they are doing or might even be able to help. Connect stakeholders with each other, because they are seeking to strengthen their networks as well. Above all, use the tools outlined in this book to prepare yourself for the next challenge.

Recall the image of the manager in the center of the organization from the introduction to this book and the environmental forces affecting that manager (shown in Figure 8.1). We now understand more about the fast-paced, complex environment that today's managers operate within, and the importance of their ability to lead work across boundaries, and to build and call on a deep network in order to achieve the best results. Keep in mind that others in this network are all also working on projects of great importance to them. In this context, it is essential that you:

- ❑ *Continue to keep good company.* Those with the strongest networks will be in the best position to garner the resources and support needed to successfully achieve their challenging goals. Be purposeful about your network and keep good company.
- ❑ *Continue to build goodwill.* Networks only matter if others are willing to participate in the projects you have. Build your reservoir of goodwill so it's there when you need it most. There will inevitably be challenging situations ahead and you can't draw upon an empty reservoir.
- ❑ *Continue to engage.* Work gets done and relationships are built through shared activities, interactions, and challenges.
- ❑ *Continue to invest in trust.* In this networked world you can't rely on control to make things happen. Trust is the essential ingredient of reliable engagement and action. Be trustworthy and respected so others will reciprocate.
- ❑ *Continue to make connections.* Leading from the center poses some unique challenges and terrific opportunities. Effectively seizing these opportunities requires that you think and act like a connector, integrator, and catalyst. Consider and understand the interdependencies, connect the right people to the work, and work simultaneously to drive results and build relationships.

BIBLIOGRAPHY

Ambady, Nalini, and Robert Rosenthal. 1992. "Thin Slices of Expressive Behavior as Predictors of Interpersonal Consequences: A Meta-Analysis." *Psychological Bulletin* 111, no. 2 (March): 256–74.

——. 1993. "Half a Minute: Predicting Teach Evaluations from Thin Slices of Nonverbal Behavior and Physical Attractiveness." *Journal of Personality and Social Psychology* 64, no. 3 (March): 431–41.

Ayer, Fred. 2001. "Collaborative Relicensing: A Success Story." *International Water Power & Dam Construction* 53, no. 1 (January): 34.

Baldwin, David, and Curt Grayson. 2004. "Influence: Gaining Commitment, Getting Results." Center for Creative Leadership Press.

Bavelas, Janet B., Linda Coates, and Trudy Johnson. 2000. "Listeners as Co-Narrators." *Mark Journal of Personality and Social Psychology* 79, no. 6 (December): 941.

Cohen, Sheldon. 2004. *"Social Relationships and Health."* American Psychologist. 59(8): 676–684 (November).

Conger, Jay. 1998. "The Necessary Art of Persuasion." *Harvard Business Review* (May-June): 84–95.

Cross, Rob and Andrew Parker. 2004. *The Hidden Power of Social Networks: Understanding How Work Really Gets Done in Organizations.* Boston, MA: Harvard Business School Press.

Denning, Stephen. 2001. *The Springboard: How Storytelling Ignites Action in Knowledge-Era Organizations.* USA: Butterworth Heinemann.

——. 2004. "Telling Tales." *Harvard Business Review* (1 May).

Eli Lilly and Company. 2004. "Achieving Value through Partnership." http://www.lilly.com/about/partnering/alliances/index .html. Accessed November.

Ganzel, Rebecca. 1999. "Telling Stories." *Presentations Magazine* (May) http://wwwpresentations.com/presentations/search/article-display.jsp.jsp?vnu_content_id=11051110.

Gardner, Howard. 1995. *Leading Minds: An Anatomy of Leadership.* New York: BasicBooks.

Gottman, John, Robert Levenson, and Erica Woodin. 2001. "Facial Expressions during Marital Conflict." *Journal of Family Communication* 1, no. 1: 37–57.

Graubard, Stephen R. 1997. "Guess Who Wasn't Invited to dinner?" *New York Times* (1 November): page A-15.

Hilgers, Laura. 2004. "Going Up?" *Attaché Magazine.* U.S. Airways (January).

Iansiti, Marco, and Roy Levien. 2004. "Strategy as Ecology." *Harvard Business Review* (March-April): 1–11.

Johnson & Johnson. 2004. "Our Company: Our Credo." (August 18, 2004.) http://www.jnj.com/our_company/our_credo/index .htm. Accessed November.

Joni, Saj-nicole A. 2004. "The Geography of Trust." *Harvard Business Review.* (March): 1–8.

Kotter, John. 1999. "What Effective General Managers Really Do." *Harvard Business Review* (March-April): 1–12.

Kouzes, James, and Barry Posner. 2003. *Credibility: How Leaders Gain and Lose It, Why People Demand It.* San Francisco: Jossey-Bass.

MacArthur, Kate. 2004. "Pepsi's Edge, Coke's C2 Get Flat Reception." *Advertising Age* 75, no. 27 (July 5): 3.

MacKenzie, Gordon. 1998. *Orbiting the Giant Hairball: A Corporate Fool's Guide to Surviving with Grace.* New York: Penguin Putnam.

Maddox, Bronwen. 2005. "All Eyes on China as G7 Passes on Africa." *The Times* (United Kingdom), 02/03/05, pg. 36.

Maister, David H., Charles H. Green, and Robert M. Galford. 2000. *The Trusted Advisor.* New York: The Free Press.

Martin, Joanne, and Melanie E. Powers. 1982. "Organizational Stories: More Vivid and Persuasive Than Quantitative Data." In *Psy-*

chological Foundations of Organizational Behavior, edited by B.M. Staw, 161–68. Glenview, Ill.: Scott, Foresman.

McKee, Robert and Bronwyn Fryer. 2003. "Storytelling That Moves People: A Conversation with Screenwriting Coach Robert McKee." *Harvard Business Review* (June).

Muoio, Anna. 1998. "The Truth Is, The Truth Hurts." *FastCompany* 14 (April): 93.

Nohria, Nitin, William Joyce, and Bruce Roberson. 2003. "What Really Works." *Harvard Business Review* (July).

Pagano, Barbara, and Elizabeth Pagano. 2004. *The Transparency Edge.* McGraw-Hill.

Pollack, Barbara. 2003. "The Art of Healing: Listening to Patients' Stories Develops Empathy." *Columbia Magazine* (Fall) http:// www.Columbia.edu/cu/alumni/Magazine?Fall2003/artofheal ing.html.

Prahalad, C.K. 2005. *The Fortune at the Bottom of the Pyramid: Eradicating Poverty through Profits.* NJ: Wharton School Publishing.

Rosner, Bob. 2004. "Gordon MacKenzie: Thinking Outside the Box." In *Minding Their Business,* interview at WorkingWounded .com.

Senge, Peter M., et al. 1994. *The Fifth Discipline Fieldbook.* New York: Doubleday.

Simmons, Annette. 2002. *The Story Factor.* Cambridge, MA: Perseus Books Group, 1st ed.

Simon, Scott. 2000. Interview with Matthew Baugh. NPR Weekend Edition. 16 December. NPR News.

Stone, Douglas, Bruce Patton, and Sheila Heen. 1999. *Difficult Conversations: How to Discuss What Matters Most.* New York: Penguin.

Tickle-Degnen, Linda, and Robert Rosenthal. 1990. "The Nature of Rapport and Its Nonverbal Correlates." *Psychological Inquiry* 1 no. 4: 285–93.

Williams, Gary A., and Robert B. Miller. 2002. "Change the Way You Persuade." *Harvard Business Review* (1 May): 1–12.

INDEX